One Way To Write

A Fast Way To Your First Book

CHARLES MUHLE

Copyright © 2011 Charles Muhel
All rights reserved.

ISBN: 0982908113
ISBN-13: 9780982908112

TwoKay Publishing
Anaheim CA
twokaybks@aol.com

Text copyright © 2011 by Charles Muhle.
Illustrations copyright © 2011 by Charles Muhle

SUMMARY: A manual that describes the basic skills needed to write and publish a first book.

Author's Note

Charles Muhle is convinced that getting a good first book published is the best way to grow any novice writer into a captivating author.

Muhle's career responsibilities included engineering, sales and marketing with prestigious electronic companies. But to relax, he wrote plays, magazine articles and stories.

The Sky Tree is his first children's story.

One Way To Write condenses the classes he took and books he read on creative writing - many of which failed to reach out to novice writers wanting to craft a first book.

In particular, this training ignored the value of an individual's style. What was needed, he felt, was a simplified way for aspiring writers to create and publish a good first book so their confidence would inspire additional books.

One Way To Write reaches out to novice writers.

Table of Contents

Introduction		ix
Step 1	Why Write	1
Step 2	What To Write	3
Step 3	The Green Book and Visit	7
Step 4	Short Stories	13
Step 5	Writer's Workshops	15
Step 6	Magazines, Digests and Books	19
Step 7	Word Processor	21
Step 8	Field Trips	25
Step 9	When and Where To Write	29
Step 10	Your Back Cover	33
Step 11	Headlines	37
Step 12	Place Map	39
Step 13	Big Bone Skeleton	49
Step 14	Characters	59
Step 15	Navigating Your Story	67
Step 16	Fine Bone Skeleton	75
Step 17	Voice and Point Of View	81

Step 18	Tell v Show		85
Step 19	The Recipe		89
Step 20	Story Spices		91
	Spice 1	Glue	91
	Spice 2	Payoff	94
	Spice 3	Tense	95
	Spice 4	Verbs	97
	Spice 5	Adverbs	97
	Spice 6	Attribution	100
	Spice 7	Exposition	102
	Spice 8	Plot Shape	105
	Spice 9	Pace	106
	Spice 10	Spacing	107
	Spice 11	Bill-boarding	108
	Spice 12	Style	110
	Spice 13	Tibs	118
	Spice 14	Illustrations	119
	Spice 15	Opening	120
	Spice 16	Acid Test	122
Step 21	Editing and Rewriting		125

Step 22	Proofreading 127
Step 23	ISBN 129
Step 24	Mock-up 131
Step 25	Agents, Publishers and POD 133
Step 26	Reference Books 137
Step 27	Our Legacies 139

APPENDIX 141

Introduction

Maybe in kindergarten you drew a picture and your parents put it up on the refrigerator under some magnets. You were proud of it then but if you drew another picture today, you know it would be better.

We all know people who say they can't draw. The truth is they can draw but don't ever try. A drawing doesn't have to look like a photograph. Instead, it can have a charming personality of its own. Your first story can also have a captivating personality if you just give it a try.

1W2W starts with your natural talent and nudges it into a story you can really be proud of. You pick a story that's fun for you to create and we use it to sharpen the skills you need to make it exciting for others.

That's the best way to prove that you really are a writer.

To simplify your first book, One Way To Write covers the key skills in small bites using a style that's informal; just like real conversation because that's what readers are into now. This is all you need for a first book. Getting it published is an event you'll always remember…even after your third book. Then, when you hear this I can't draw or I can't write stuff, you'll smile and think,

'Sure you can…but you have to try.'

When I use an example from The Sky Tree to illustrate a style or skill, I include that section in 1W2W for your quick reference. But for best results, you should look for other examples in your own copy of The Sky Tree and highlight them with your own notes.

As the title 1W2W implies, there are other ways to write. Our mission is to get a first story written and published because this is the best way to discover YW2W…Your Way To Write your next book.

STEP 1
Why Write

Writing creative fiction is waiting for you.

"Hey, over here. In your brain. See that door you never tried? Go ahead, open it. Inside there's a big room with ten doors and each door has another ten behind it. All of the doors grant you a wish. After all, this is creative city.

"You can go through as many doors as you want and pick any wish you like. But do the rest of us a favor and tell us about who you meet, what they did, any problems that showed up and how it all turned out."

"Hmm, so many doors. Thriller, SciFi, Romance, Mystery, Humor."

This is a room we all carry around in that space above our necks and below our hair. Now we are going to look inside and learn how to shape what we find into the story you always wanted to write.

One of the benefits of taking up golf is you can enjoy the sport even in your declining years. Well, writing is even more enduring. You can enjoy writing even after you can't swing a golf club, when it's raining, when it's dark and when you're ninety-five... and there are no green fees.

There are lots of exercises for your body but not too many that stretch your brain. For a well-balanced life, you need both. Stress is a covert agent bent on destroying health and shortening life. Writing stops stress build-up by focusing on wonderful new characters and plots for you, the boss, to describe and share.

Being in charge with no constraints is a trip you'll never forget. Take one trip and you'll take more and each one gets better.

I guarantee you that when you start your story it will consume every spare mental moment. Time spent at the keyboard will pass at the speed of light. You'll look at the clock and wonder where the last four hours went.

Creative writing becomes a personal passion that can be expanded, changed and improved even while you're waiting in a checkout line.

How about that bedtime story you made up once for a five year old. Wouldn't it be great to share it with every five year old in the world?

How can you not try writing?

STEP 2
What To Write

Most people feel creative writing is really difficult.

That's because our early experience with writing was not fun; like writing a thank you note to grandma, writing a story in school when you knew everything you put down was going to be "examined" for accuracy and the rules of grammar. "Jeesh! Let's get this over with."

Later, you "had" to write home because you needed money. Or maybe you had a complaint about how your order got screwed up by a department store.

But technology has changed feelings about writing. It's fun to text or e-mail friends and family. Keyboard and thumbing skills just happened to us overnight. Today, writing is more like hanging out. Now, when we get an idea or news, we can share it easily.

We all have read books that were great and not so great. When we finish a good book, we take a deep breath and look forward to talking about the story with someone who also read it.

A few books later, we think maybe WE could write a book. Even a great book, maybe. But then our early history kicks in and we remember when Miss Evans trashed our story?

Get real.

But the thought doesn't go away. We get a job or two or three. We get other priorities like spouse(s), kid(s), house(s), car(s). Life is complex.

Finally, when we get good enough at managing the life we created, we fill our spare time with hobbies like kayaking, guitar, camping, and cruising.

We dally in these fresh pastimes until their newness wears thin then we look for a new diversion. Something original, maybe; creative even. "Hmm? Let's see. I wonder if I have a book inside of me? I could write it in some spare moments, even at five a.m. I could work out some plot thoughts on my commute. Spell check will catch any goofs. Maybe I should give it a shot. It's gotta be more convenient than camping.

"Think I'll hit the library and see what the creative-writing books advise. Wow, look at them all. Some are pretty thick. This gal has twenty-three best sellers and says it's easy. This book is by an English Lit Professor. Here are six books on dialogue alone. Maybe I'll go camping instead."

The steep learning curve is a turn-off.

What new authors need is a simplified guide for creating and publishing a first book; a guide that is easy to understand and enjoyable to follow because there's no steep learning curve.

1W2W shows you how to build a story frame (the melody) that is strong enough to hold conflict, growth and drama (the harmony) and make you…an author.

So how do we get started with the melody?

STEP 3
The Green Book and Visit

Look at these answers and tell me what the question is?

A diamond, a dog and a journal.

The question is:

What is the best friend of a girl, a man and a writer?

No tool is more valuable to you as a writer than a journal.

The computer is a close second but the journal is easier to carry everywhere, to jot an idea into, to capture a happening and to make good use of a few minutes while waiting for the movie to start.

You can do all this with a laptop computer but not as easily. The journal is not used to write your story; it's used to capture the illusive ideas you set free in your creative room. Ideas can pop up at any place and at any time so you need to carry your new pal everywhere. For me, a six by nine inch spiral notebook works well. Mine is **green**. It's not too geeky looking and lies flat when I write a note in it.

I suggest you number every page in your '**Green Book**' and jot your notes and ideas on only the odd pages (or even pages) so you can add printouts, clippings and related info near note context that makes the most sense. A folded 8.5 by 11 inch printout can also be added conveniently to this size book.

Your journal is now your new and private best friend.

And here's the only rule in 1W2W:

Do not show your Green Book notes to anyone because other eyeballs chill or kill your creativity.

Start right away to make a short entry every day even if you have nothing more to write than:

Sept 17, 2011- as my first writing project, I think I'll write a story about a dog named Skipper who saved a boy's life.

Such uninhibited entries soon become a natural habit and you're more likely to add creative thoughts about plots and characters and since you know no one else gets to see your notes, even crazy scenes.

Write anything you feel because it's feelings that will make your story captivating. Right now you are just getting comfortable with putting gut feelings onto paper but once this is as natural as scratching an itch, your creative thoughts will get captured in the full color of YOUR style and you *become* the character of your story.

Now you and your new best friend are ready to decide what kind of story you want to begin with.

Since you will be learning many new skills, I suggest you start with a children's book, a young adult book or a fantasy to simplify your first project. These kinds of stories give you the most freedom to create intriguing characters and cool plots. In addition, you can invent any magical possibility you want to make your story exciting.

If you pick a mature theme for your first book, your reader will expect some of the characters to engage in intimate lovemaking. Writing sex scenes is extremely difficult for both first time writers and experienced writers. If you doubt this, try writing a scene or two before deciding what kind of story to start with. You may need to study how other writers handle these scenes in order to blend your versions gracefully into your story.

The Sky Tree is neither a blockbuster best seller nor a mature adventure novel. It's a charming children's story about a whimsical dreamer. Since you will be learning many new skills with your first book, a simple story works best.

Whatever you decide, you'll find that 1W2W "advice" applies to all kinds of fiction. You'll learn so much from this system, you'll start looking forward, just like I did, to your next book.

But hold off on picking a story type until after... **The Visit**

Yes, you and your new green-book-best-friend now need to VISIT your local bookstore to shake hands with the real world.

The competition is severe. As you browse through the different sections like SciFi, Mystery, Adventure, Children's, take notes on page count, word count, type size, book size (called Trim), number and types of illustrations. Notice that, in many children's books, the drawings are simple black and white stick figures. Nothing elaborate is needed because kids love to imagine.

Buy one or two books that match your first book. These "models" will help you form ideas for your cover, title, sub-title, ISBN page, contents, chapter headings and other items like the author's bio, dedication, acknowledgements, forward, introduction, prologue, story and epilogue.

As you read 1W2W, keep the model book handy so you can see how the model's author handles things like attribution, adverbs, pace, exposition etc. Then you can better decide what works best for YOU.

Your VISIT shows you many possible models for your first book but remember that our mission is:

To learn the new skills while writing an exciting story

To bring your first book all the way to publication

To answer the question, "Am I an author?"

To accomplish these objectives, pick a first story that lets you concentrate *most* on learning the new skills.

Now you know why I picked a children's story.

STEP 4
Short Stories

Start-up-writers often find it's tempting to get involved in writing short stories because their brevity seems more manageable. But that brevity is also daunting because you do not have enough "space" to set the scene, expose needed background information, make conflict seem real or paint the personalities completely.

While any writing helps develop your skill, very short stories are more difficult to write than a 4,000 word story. Can they be "great?' Sure, but rarely because they do not have lots of character interaction and…

dialogue is THE key to believability.

STEP 5
Writer's Workshops

New writers are also attracted to professional writer organizations – either by joining one or attending a weekend conference. Certainly, these can be enjoyable and informative but they can also be overwhelming because they present accomplished authors who use a variety of styles and skills.

Often the wanna-be author enjoys the stimulation but is also shocked by how much she or he needs to learn to become a "real author." So there is a danger that these events can intimidate more than inspire. It's more important that, as a new author, you find and nourish your own style first because that is what will keep you writing and make your stories captivating.

New authors can locate their own style only…by writing.

That's why, in the beginning, writing a first book is more important than joining a professional organization.

Start-up writers also find it tempting to join a writer's workshop group. After all we writers are so hard to find. But these well-meaning groups often are NOT effective for advancing *your style* of writing. For example, there are strong and not so strong personalities in any group that can unbalance the rapport and intimidate a novice.

Or if member A writes cryptic prose, he or she is unlikely to get helpful suggestions from member B who writes in a flowery style. Is that any good for anyone?

Or, too much time is spent on some trivial grammatical item like where a word should be hyphenated. Usually this is just a showboat display of one's educational quality.

Or. Member C likes to read her poetry and none of the others even like poems. How do we tell her enough already? We don't. They may be beautiful poems but you want to write stories in your style because you sense, correctly,

the clothes of those other styles just do not fit you.

And as for debating the rules of grammar, let me make a point on why they're not the big deal now that they were when Bill Shakespeare was writing. Are thou listening?

Supposing your boss Tom wants to give you some work related advice after you start working with him. He invites you to grab a sandwich over by Pearson Park, sit on a bench and just chat about work. Both of you realize this is a non-trivial conversation so you listen to every word he says. In fact some of his comments cause you to stop eating your BLT.

All of a sudden, this homeless guy runs up to you two and points across the street at the bank and grunts, "Hey, deez two guys jes run into the bank wid guns and masks, ya know?"

Both of you forget whatever you were talking about and lock onto this guy's story.

Do either one of you even notice the guy's grammar? No. You're both totally captivated by the dramatic event.

There was a time, a long time ago, when beautiful prose and faultless grammar were essential and even glorified but dem days are gone. Today's fiction has to be written in the idiom of real world characters.

Your job is to get exciting conflict and drama onto paper in a way that's believable.

So if workshops or classes don't give you incisive commentary on your particular style and you really don't like the other creations that much, you're better off learning about POV, exposition, voice etc. from inside your own story instead of trying to blend conflicting suggestions from others into your story.

By the third workshop meeting, you're thinking about all the other things you'd rather be doing and by the fourth meeting, you're sorry but you have to drop out because "you're moving to Alaska."

You can't drive to your unique excellence if you let others do the steering.

When you write the way YOU feel, your creativity is maximized, you want to keep writing and because your readers sense the soul you share, they lock onto your story like it's their own breathing.

And most of us enjoy breathing.

STEP 6
Magazines, Digests and Books

For those of us who get the urge to write, it's natural to be attracted to writer's magazines and How-To-Write books. I've learned a lot from these publications where experienced authors share ideas that are profound and practical.

But talented artists are not necessarily the best instructors. Their art comes easy to them so it's hard for them to relate to less gifted creators. If a renowned oil painter writes a book on how to be a masterful oil painter, do you think it would help you become one? I don't think so. Sure you would develop artistic sensitivity about oil paintings but it would help you more if the book showed ways to enhance *your own* style not how to copy the artist's style.

These magazines and How-To books can be helpful…

But not if they convince you that writing is too complex to even try.

It isn't complex at all especially if you stay true to your personal feelings and not try to copy an author you might admire. Our OWN expressions on paper are what we need to create.

New writers also look through Writer Digests that contain all the publishers, their rules and rates. Do not let all these do's and don'ts scare you off. Book publishing is going through a digital sea-change right now that may leave some publishers and their rules high and dry. Think newspapers.

Few publishers welcome unproven talent. How bout none!

Our goal is to write a finished book in our own style while learning how to blend all the skills that make it exciting, enjoyable and captivating.

You can't learn how to ice skate from a book. You have to put on skates and try. 1W2W laces up your skates to get your characters, plot, conflicts and drama into YOUR book and get you onto the ice.

You will learn a lot from writing your first book. You will know yourself better, know what story you want to write next, know the structure of characters, scenes, chapters, and tension and also know what you did well and what you need to tune up.

Writing a book is the best way to find out if you really are an author

STEP 7
Word Processor

Let me cut to the chase.

You need to use a word processor if you want to write a book.

Computers are not expensive now. Brand new mini computers called Netbooks sell for around $300 and come with the popular word processor named Word made by Microsoft. You need these tools to write your book.

Many older computers get replaced by the latest and greatest new systems every month so you can easily find a perfectly good, used computer for a super low price. The seller will usually throw in software at no charge. Just be sure the SW ownership rights get transferred properly.

For the people that claim they can't draw or can't handle new technology, shame on them for not trying. There are plenty of daughters, sons, nieces, nephews and neighbor kids that can bring you up to speed on a word processor in less than an hour. So give them $21.00 to join the 21st century.

Tell them you're going to write a book. They'll love to help.

You don't even HAVE to connect your computer to the Internet to create your book. You can just use it only as a smart typewriter because it's easier to operate than a typewriter. The spell-checking alone will save you hours.

But the Internet will save you months of research. Like what size bullet does your hero need for his Glock. And how many Glock models are there? He picked a Glock G20 over a Glock G37 because...?

How many eyes does a spider have? What's the runway length of the airport nearest to Cartersvill, Montana? Good luck without the Internet.

You will need a printer also. A brand new one can be yours for around $80. This equipment can be legitimately written off for paying bills on-line, for tracking your portfolio or whatever else you do for a living - like becoming an author.

Now you own the most powerful tools since the printing press.

The music industry has already gone digital; newspapers too and movies and TV. Books are next. Think Kindle and iPads. Social communication is mostly digital. The good news for authors is that this new digital age makes it *easier* for a first time writer to launch a first book using an e-Publisher like Createspace, the outfit owned by Amazon.

STEP 8
Field Trips

Here are some fun ways to get your creative room ready for your characters.

Take a bus trip with your (green?) journal and write about the people that get on and off. Capture impressions of face, body, behavior, dress, mood, how they pick a seat, anything memorable. Be sure to make up a name for each character.

Go to Walmart to people-watch and describe them. Stroll to a quiet spot and scribble some notes like you're checking prices. Ask a "Sales Associate" a question and tell your green book about how it was answered. Just a few key words are needed. Write down a name for each character.

These trips help us capture observations, descriptions, reactions, characterizations, feel, ambiance in...

a notebook that no one but you will ever see.

Green book trips also help push open the door to your creativity room. The more often you push, the easier it is to invent character types that your readers find intriguing.

Visit a "fishing" pier to describe the people. Talk to them. They may NOT be what you expected. Ask, "What's the best time to fish out here?" They will enjoy sharing their wisdom. Name the people.

Visit a park and describe how the pigeons or ducks argue over a peanut. Which one is the dominant bird? Name it. Which one is number two? Name it.

Describing your story characters in a unique, catchy way is hard. It's common to describe hair color, eye color, height and weight. These are un-remarkable tags for the reader. How about, "His left eye looks off to the side like he's about to lie."

This might not be great but it is memorable and can be mentioned later in your story, "As soon as he started to tell me what happened, his left eye drifted off again." Boy, we remember this guy.

Or how about this for a womanizer?

> "So you think your friend Marvin is always looking to hook up?"

> "Well, he keeps his rear view mirror pointed sharply at the next lane so he can check out the lady drivers. So whad'a you think?"

We didn't tell our reader he was a womanizer, we "showed" what a womanizer he is with dialogue. Now later when we describe Marvin's slick-backed, greasy hair, we remember this guy.

Describe your characters and places using all five senses.

Sight   tall, slim, clothes, neat, age, clean, beard, glasses, shoes, rings, ear shape, haircut, tics.

Smell   aftershave, cigarettes, breath, perfume, car scent, popcorn, bakery, hot wet pavement, garlic.

Hearing   Loud, gravel voice, breathing, denture whistle, street noise, silence, running water, elevator swish, echo, public announcement. What he told you and how. Is she sorry she hit the dog? Is he proud he lied to his buddy? How often does he use "I" did this or that?

Feel   handshake, temperature, escalator lift, wind, carpet, upholstery, al dente, crisp, bumpy road, gooey, sticky, damp.

Taste   salty, sweet, spicy, bitter, bland.

Next time you're in a supermarket, look at the guy's shopping cart and try to figure out how many people live with him, who does the cooking, does he have a pet, guess how old he is. Give him a name.

We put all this stuff in our green book because:

observation is the best friend of creativity and we want both to be habit forming.

We authors need to keep pushing on the door to our creative room.

STEP 9
When and Where To Write

When I walk into a bookstore, I pause inside the door because I'm not quite sure what books I might be interested in right now. The mood I'm in needs nourishment but I just finished *Doctor Mary's Monkey* so no more heavy stuff for a few weeks.

Our mood influences what we want to read next.

Your mood also needs to be respected when you are about to work on your first book. A mood of introspection inspires whimsical fresh creativity and a mood of logic deals best with organizing the words and chapters you've already written.

My creative moments show up in the early morning. That's when I write new copy. Later in the day, I'll do manuscript housekeeping like spell checking, re-arranging paragraphs, some rewriting and other less creative book needs.

When you start your writing day, it's tempting to "fix up" paragraph three or re-order the chapters because it's easy to see what needs doing and just do it.

Don't go there when you're in a fresh, creative mood.

Instead, write the next new chapter.

Three weeks later you may decide to junk that paragraph or chapter you were going to tune up.

Do the hard (creative) stuff when you mind is fresh and do the easy (housekeeping) stuff when your brain is low on gas.

When your first draft of your book is done, it will be easy to tell what needs to be fixed, re-arranged, augmented or tossed.

Where To Write

Creative thought is the most essential element of good fiction and also the most difficult to capture so we need find a place that helps us coach it out into the open. Maybe that place is your home office while you sip tea and write. But you might find sitting in a quiet park near a lake helps you create too. Or the bookish ambiance of a library. Or a chapel. Or the seashore. Try some different places to see if they help you discover fresh approaches to your story line and style.

The scenes in your book start with an idea then what must happen, what could happen and what DID happen (maybe surprisingly). You can capture these elements in your green book or laptop no matter where you are but you may find certain locations stimulate creative thought best.

STEP 10
Your Back Cover

Here's the back cover for *The Sky Tree*.

> A young squirrel named Minty is captivated
> by a dream of visiting a giant tree that touches
> the clouds. On the way, she and her friend,
> Darrin, learn of the dreams of others while
> facing the dangers of the wild like the Mangler
> Ants that guard Angry Island.

Now it's time for you to write a back cover blurb for *your* story.

Make it as long as you want because at this stage we are capturing thoughts. They are hard to see and they fly fast. Capture all of them and **then** select the keepers.

Write your cover blurb on your computer and put every version in your green book so you can see the progress you make when you change it nine times.

If your back cover doesn't "hook" good, write another one or pick another title and keep cycling until something clicks with your mood. Save ALL of the versions. If there are two ideas that look good to you, write back covers for both. Tomorrow, you'll know which one you really want to use.

Aren't you glad no one sees the stuff you are coming up with?

By now you may agree that the creative boulder is the hardest thing to go over on our story journey. That's why a Sci-Fi or kid's story has so much appeal. There are no constraints on what can happen. A talking chimp that finds a cell phone may be a fun first story. After all, our mission is to get a story written and published so we can show agents, publishers and ourselves we can do it.

Your finished book on Amazon is a great selling tool for your *next* book and a thousand times more effective than sending an unsolicited manuscript to a publisher or agent.

Back to *The Sky Tree*...So I'm okay with my back cover. The Mangler Ants suggest all sorts of conflict. That's usually a good hook. Now all I have to do is hassle my little friends as they head for the tall tree.

Truth time. My first draft of *The Sky Tree* (I named that version *The Sequoia*) was so bad I was ashamed I had shared it with a few friends and I was determined to fix it. But as bad as it was, it provided me a detailed synopsis that I could use as the skeleton of a **good** story. My rewrite flowed so effortlessly, I was convinced it was due to the sequence of Title, Back Cover and (synopsis) Skeleton.

By accident, I had stumbled across 1 Way 2 Write.

To help visualize my story, I doodled a map that proved so helpful I revised it as the story "talked to me". I put the final version of the map right at the front of my book so browsers and readers would feel they already know the place where Minty lived. Take a peek at the map of Misty Valley.

STEP 11
Headlines

Now we need to expand our back cover summary using headlines which cover who, what, when, where and why.

Please see all of the original headlines for *The Sky Tree* in the appendix as they were created in July of 2010. Notice that some names and events have been changed for the book version.

For *The Sky Tree,* the latest headlines are:

> Minty learns that a baby crow hurt her wing
> Minty sees a tall tree that touches the clouds
> She finds Darrin who also wants to visit the clouds
> Darrin learns how to sneak-climb
> They get advice from a Wrinkly about visiting the Sky Tree
> On the way, they meet a beaver family with a problem.
> A lady rabbit helps the dreamers cross Batwing Field

Headlines are easy to expand, re-arrange or toss before you do ANY writing. They also tell you if you even have a story. If not, it's back to your creative room. At least you haven't wasted three months of writing.

Headlines also help you work efficiently because when you start your writing day, you can pick out the headlines that fit the mood you happen to be in and write them well.

At this point you should have a back cover and some headlines written. Maybe even two or three back covers with headlines for each one. This exercise helps make what you read next in 1W2W more meaningful because you can relate the advice to your own story ideas.

STEP 12
Place Map

Maybe brilliant authors do not need any help developing exciting plot lines or memorable characters but I sure do.

Where do I begin?

Do I invent fascinating characters and then describe how they handle events. Or do I invent a string of hair-raising events and plug in the characters?

YES is the answer to both questions. These two story ingredients are attached at the hip so the problem is which one to start with. We just need to do SOMETHING.

As a child, did you ever look at the clouds and try to imagine what objects or animals the clouds looked like? Pretty easy because visualization and imagination are cousins. Using both helps us to create.

Lets play with a kindergarten drawing. Take a blank sheet of paper and draw a straight line across the middle of the sheet (Portrait or landscape is okay).

What is that line? Is it the horizon of the ocean where they caught the monster octopus? Or is it the top of a dam that's about to fail and flood the village? Or maybe it's a bullet zinging through the air at the hero or villain?

Throw the sheet away to prove that no one else gets to see any of your creative thoughts. But remember how easy it was to "imagine" what thoughts a simple line might trigger.

Our sight stimulates our imagination and we need all the help we can get to create. Watch how it helps when we re-start *The Sky Tree*. Get a new sheet of paper and join me when I draw a vertical line to be Minty's Pine tree. Scratch in a few branches on the right and left. Now where is her nest? On the right? Where's the crow's nest? Same level? Higher? What's at the base of the tree? Rocks? Bushes?

We start our first book with a tantalizing back cover blurb. We build headlines to make bite-sized events we can play with to add excitement. Next, we sketch a diagram or map of where our story begins.

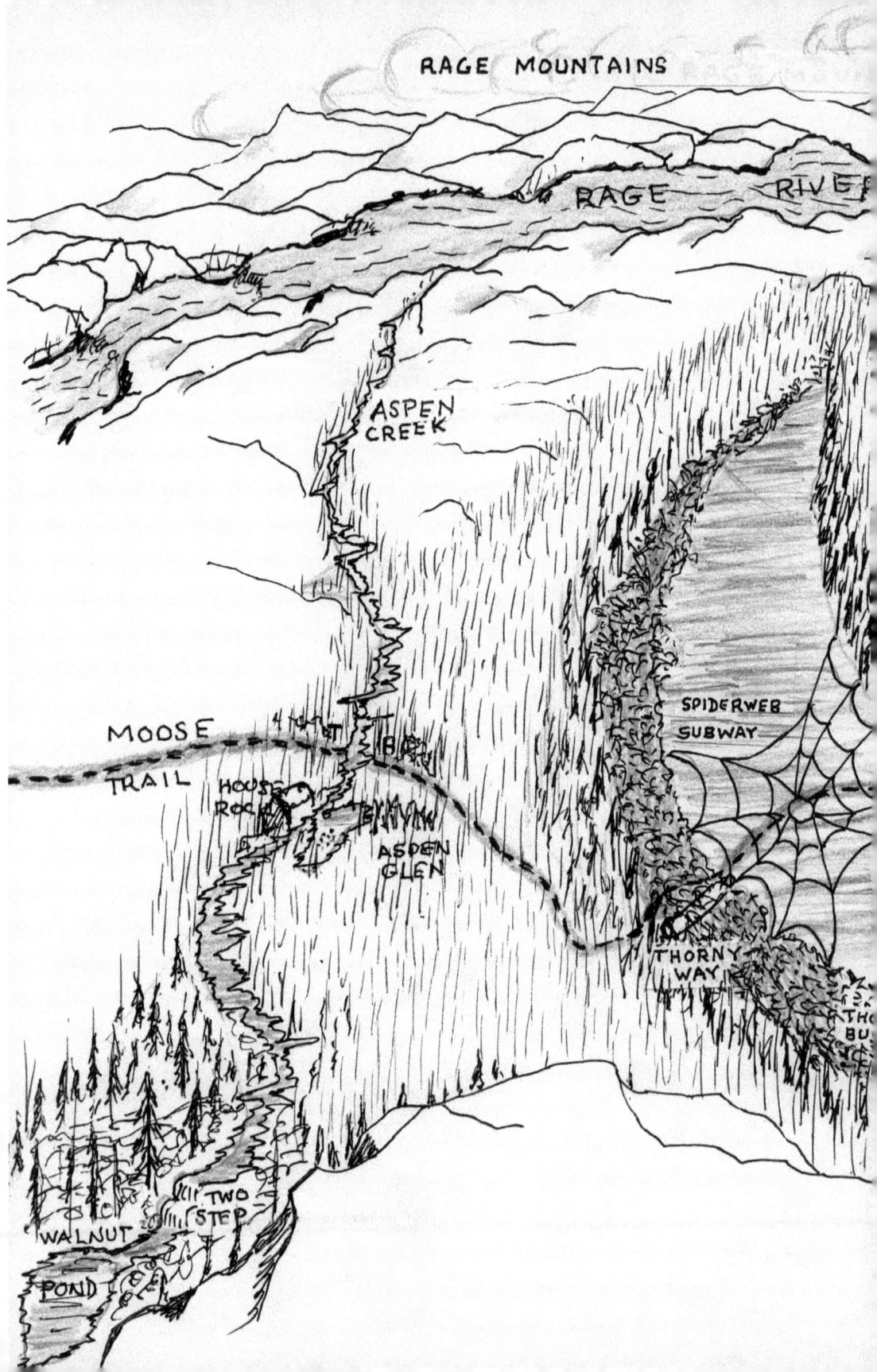

On *The Sky Tree* map of Misty Valley, I put Minty's nest tree near Walnut Pond and, diagonally across from it, I put Angry Island, the home of the Sky Tree.

Immediately, I started visualizing where creeks and rivers should be. Next I added a path for Minty and Darrin to follow. They hike past beaver pond, some thorny bushes and (under) big, open Batwing Field. It was easy to invent characters and problems along the way. As I needed to add obstacles for Minty, I sketched them on the map. What you're looking at is the fifth version of my map.

A rough map for your story can help you visualize ideas also. And if it helps *you* visualize, it will also help *your reader*s to connect with your story too so give serious thought to including a place map in your book.

And next time you're in a library or bookstore, take a look at the James A. Michener's *Alaska, Chesapeake, The Source, Texas* and other stories that have his maps right up front.

Now why would a famous author do that?

To help the writer or help the reader?

Yes.

Your sketch is just a device to get your creative juices flowing so don't worry about how good it is. Just doodle some lines.

Let's look at how a sketch or diagram might help your creativity for the following made-up titles.

What to look for in a ten-speed

Sketch a bike and the seat, brake grips, clip peddles, helmet, gloves, what size tires, what make of bike, type of lights. Think of its best feature (weight?) and its worst (spare parts availability).

The Hacker Wizard

Doodle a guy at a computer. Young or old? Desk top? Laptop? Only one or several? A poster on the wall? Beard? A beer or coffee nearby?

Campsite Killer

Plot the RV park. Twisted trails and paths? Show where the bad guy sleeps and where the first victim's RV is parked. Is it near bad guy or on the other side of the camp? Where's the rest room-shower shed?

We don't care how good your sketches are. Your doodling provokes visualization and lets you look around the campsite and see the broken tree branch. What's that all about?

Then your imagination kicks in. That poster on the killer's wall...is it Charles Manson or Mickey Mouse? At this point in time we're not sure but we are thinking up creative possibilities faster than we can write them down in our green book.

Here's another example of how a doodle map provokes creativity.

Say we want to write a story about a rich rancher whose wife has died. He misses her a lot. There are ranch hands around but no one lives with him in the big house and he's lonely. His sister in New York is married to this successful Wall street guy. They have a teenage son who is always in trouble. Their marriage sucks so she decides to take her juvie son to live on the ranch. Get the kid out of the city and take a break from broker-guy. The brother is thrilled to have some family to chat with and maybe he can straighten the kid out.

We doodle out a map of the ranch, where the two grazing valleys are, the canyon and the river bend where the kid becomes a hero.

For the house, we doodle a cube, rectangle? U-Shape? Where are the barns? Two story? Trees?

For the kitchen, we show that this one has a fireplace (!) and that's where the kid breaks the bottle or ???

So we just relax and doodle so our creativity gets involved. And we let it. We have lots of paper so we take any scene, doodle it and new things that HAVE to be there pop into our minds.

Draw a sketch or map of your opening scene. What kind of stuff has to be there? What is there that is a surprise? And since no

One Way To Write

one is going to see any of this stuff, anything is okay to include for this creative trip we're on.

Don't throw it away yet. Date it and put it in a pile or file we'll call Stack. Like a Push-Down stack that has the most recent item on top. Tossing this stuff later is easy. Thinking it up to begin with is the hard part.

But not any more.

Now as you add story headlines and events take a peek at the sketch and "imagine" details you might want to add or re-draw.

STEP 13
Big Bone Skeleton

Once you have a created:

    the blurb for the back cover of your book

    headlines that add main events to the cover story

    sketches of places (and maybe characters)

you need to build a body for your story. So we start with the big bones of the plot skeleton. Don't worry about punctuation or spelling when you're turning headlines into big bones.

Here's the skeleton for *The Sky Tree*.

    In a Pine tree nest, Minty is born as two bees watch
    She's a curious little gal; sleeps on mint leaves
    Later, she notices a crow's nest in the same tree
    Her Mom climbs down and spots a bear cub
    She lures the cub away from the nest tree

> Days later, Minty sees a tall tree far away
> It actually touches the clouds
> She's excited, wants to climb it
> Mom tells her about the tree's legend
> Now, she really wants to visit it

Lets pause here to see who's going to tell this story?

> The Mom? - "I was waiting to give birth…"

> Minty? – "I was born a year ago…"

> True Bees? – We watched the nest for days…"

Someone has to be telling the story. Whoever it is sees everything that happens in the tree and on the ground. Some "voice" seems to know all the details. This is called the omnipotent point of view, (OPOV). This see-all, know-all POV is comfortable for your reader to follow and it's easy for you to use too.

Lets look at the start of *The Sky Tree…*

> Halfway up the nearest Pine, a pair of True Bees waits for the birth of a baby squirrel. Their big eyes never blink and their see-through wings are still. They don't mind waiting because it is their job to spread the news when a baby is born. And they love their job.
>
> A few weeks earlier, Diaza and Kazo waited in the same tree for two baby crows to arrive. They watched the white eggs with dark spots for

the first nip of an egg tooth. Then they buzzed through the forest to tell all the animals and trees about Chakra and Crawford.

Diaza sees something move up in the crow's nest. She points her antenna and whispers, "Kazo, look at that Chakra. She's gonna fall, for sure."

Kazo flicks his antenna but doesn't need to move his head to see Chakra swaying on oversized feet and flapping fluff covered wings. "She should know better…Oh my, she's falling."

Chakra falls, bumps off a small twig and summersaults onto a soft raspberry bush near the stream below. More frightened than hurt; she crawls under a clump of grass near the falls and stays quiet.

"Quick, Kazo, go get her mom."

"You go. I'll wait for the new baby squirrel."

"No. You go and I'll let you do all the telling about the new baby."

"Okay, it's a deal." Off he buzzes.

The OPOV lets an author jump into actual dialogue and back into OPOV in a smooth way that readers find natural.

Once we get our readers really interested in our story, we do NOT want to jolt them with anything that distracts them from their mental ride-along. Here, we are asking them to pretend that bees talk, for example, and we need to write in a way that preserves the favor the readers are doing us.

Just to see a different POV. Here's the first paragraph using a first person POV (FPOV) of one of the bees.

> Halfway up the nearest Pine, I was waiting with my friend for the birth of a baby squirrel. We are True Bees. Our big eyes never blink and see-through wings are still. We don't mind waiting because it is our job to spread the news when a baby is born. And we love our job.

Does this version seem as smooth?

> "Our big eyes never blink and our see-through wings are still?"

You can write your story using a FPOV but it's not as easy as the OPOV. For example, the FPOV can't relate what the other character is thinking.

However, the FPOV does deliver a HUGE amount of believability because it reads like a dairy.

When you write your story you could use OPOV all the time or jump to FPOV for the main character for some chapters. Just make sure your POV switch does not jolt your reader. Changing the POV at a new chapter is smooth because your reader is okay with a new viewpoint at the start of a new chapter.

Detective stories often use FPOV for the main cop and OPOV for the other parts.

Since we want to keep our learning slope gentle, I suggest you write your first story using the OPOV.

By the way, did you notice how easily we got dragged in to the discussion of POV and Tense? It's hard to talk about one element of the writing craft without mentioning how it relates to another. You almost need a recipe.

Now we need to create a big bone (synopsis) skeleton with no dialogue, just all of the events that happen. This lets us get our whole story (plan) down on "paper". Then we can easily insert some surprises, tune it with some small bone details and then dress our skeleton with the feelings and motivations of our players.

Lets look at another skeleton example to see how to bring in conflict and drama.

> Ken meets Tanya

Now we need conflict

> Ken meets Tanya
> Tanya already has a boyfriend named Brandon Cooper

Now we need drama

> Ken meets Tanya
> Tanya already has a boyfriend named Brendon Cooper
> Brandon is Ken's boss

Now we need to hang flesh on our skeleton for the start of our story.

But first, let's draw a map of a major street (Broadway) across a sheet of paper and a minor street (Maple) that intersects it at a right angle. Just to the right of the intersection, on Broadway, is a low hedge. Behind the hedge, a motorcycle cop watches the stop sign on Maple. Our story begins…

> Officer Ken Mason likes the thick hedge near the stop sign. Late-for-work drivers rarely look to the right. The chest high hedge hides his motorcycle but not his view. Mason just sits back on the saddle and folds his arms. He's careful not to touch the sharp creases of his blue uniform. He knows by noon, he'll be wishing he'd worn his tans.
>
> Right now, his only challenge is to decide when is a stop really a stop and not a slow glide through the intersection.
>
> Over the hedge he sees a yellow Honda; a customer, maybe? Nope. Honda boy actually stops then heads up Broadway. Ken watches him pass. Kid must be barely twenty. Music blaring.
>
> Quiet again. Best part of his day is the morning briefing. Cop humor is so twisted. Especially Romaro's stuff. Ken is smiling as a red Mustang rolls through the stop and, with a short tire squeak, heads up Broadway
>
> He punches the starter, gets a purr and thinks Lady Customer, here I come.
>
> He lights up the red spots and rolls after her.

> She doesn't pull over right away and his amusement morphs into annoyance. He's sure she sees the spots. The Mustang slows to a stop, motor on. He brakes, touches down his boot heel and kicks out the stand. Kills the motor. Blue flashers still on.
>
> Studied calm movement as he approaches. "Morning, Miss. Could I see your license and registration, please."
>
> A nod and half smile, "Officer, you happen to know Lieutenant Cooper?"

Now we can expand this sample of conflict into drama when Cooper later learns Ken gave his girlfriend Tanya a ticket. Does he chew him out? Change his beat? Glare at him silently.? What happens at the annual softball outing when Ken heads for home and Cooper is behind home plate catching the throw-in from third?

He spikes Ken! Cuts him on the arm.

You can mine this vein further. Cooper is way too possessive of Tanya and she's a little fed up with that. Ken seemed kinda nice and he's hot too. So one early morning when Ken and Tanya happen to meet at a local gym, she asks Ken what Cooper did to him. He won't tell her but said it was childish. Later she finds out from another cop what happened at the softball game and she's really ticked.

Next time at the gym, she sorta apologizes for Cooper. Ken and Tanya start seeing each other and Cooper starts checking on her. Cooper's got a BIG ego problem and he's a little crooked too.

One cozy night, Tanya tells Ken of some shady dealings at the station's evidence room. Ken looks into it (almost gets caught) and it is serious. Now we have a three-way clash that could go anywhere.

We started with Ken meets Tanya and added conflict and then drama. It isn't difficult if you push the door to your creative room open, squeeze inside and look around. I find "looking around" comes easier with a doodle map or sketch. It helps me picture the hedge, stop sign, tire squeak, music, temperature, boot heel, engine purr, blue lights.

And when I'm nursing creativity out of its hiding places, I need all the help I can get.

If you were going to build a house, you'd think about where to build (Place Map), about room count (back cover), about a floor-plan (headlines), about kitchen layout (skeletons), about colors (dressing the skeletons) and about the resulting ambiance (your finished book).

For sure, you would use lots of sketches to help you picture the house. You'd throw some sketches away and draw more and you would do all this without thinking because this is a natural way to capture creative thoughts so others share in them. You never even think of saying, "I can't draw."

Writing your first book is nowhere near as difficult as designing your first house. You just do the same things. And you don't need to pay for any changes you make because YOU are the designer and the builder of your book.

And best of all, the project costs you...nothing.

The Dream Journey

Early in 1849, in a small village east of Cleveland, Ohio, there was a problem.

Many of the young men and women who dreamed of starting their own farm, raising a family and leaving a legacy found little opportunity for all that. So when they heard that out west you could start your own spread by pounding stakes in the ground, ten couples decided to form a wagon train and trek 2500 miles west where fertile valleys waited.

When they started their trip, no one had any real idea what they would end up creating. Often they had to backtrack and try a different trail. Their trek was sometimes tiring, sometimes exciting. Along the way, they debated if they should stick with the original plan or embrace surprise opportunities.

At mile 852, the wagon train cut through a narrow canyon and found a wide river flowing south. Two couples decided to stop there and build their future around the river trade. At mile 1336, three couples decided to stop near the lush green foothills and raise cattle. The remaining couples traveled 312 miles to reach the west coast just in time to join the gold rush.

As an author, you will find the same choices. You start with a rough idea of where your story and characters are headed. But as you turn corners in your plot, surprises materialize and they may be more exciting than your original plot. The writing journey itself encourages your creativity to rush ahead and invent possibilities. What's around the next corner? This trail doesn't look promising. Should I backtrack here and regroup?

Unpredictable twists are natural to any trip. Pause your trip long enough to "taste" the surprises. Play 'What if?' Jot down some 'other ways to go from here.' What twist could I inject here that would pull my reader in an exciting direction never expected.

You already did this when you added twists in your headlines that were not really in your back cover blurb. Your new adventure will not soar if you keep it tethered an outline.

If your story tugs you in a direction that you didn't anticipate, go there for a while. See what's around the corner. It may be golden. You can always backtrack if the side trip is bland. It's okay not to know exactly what's going to happen next. Your creativity wants to help you write an exciting story. Let it happen.

Save your new thoughts and ideas (journal or computer) so you can decide later if they are goofy or golden.

STEP 14
Characters

Name, Growth and First Appearance

Names

You can't believe how much time we can waste picking out the names of our characters. So stop writing, go to the nearest bookstore and get a book on names. Do not even stop to get your green book. That's how important this step is.

Do not rely on the Internet for this. You need to flip pages, scan names, compare four or five and pick one. Does it have to be THE perfect name right now? No. We need to get on with our writing. By the time that's done you will know exactly what end-name is right so don't waste creative time on the jitter of name picking. Even a perfect name may HAVE to be changed by chapter six.

I find it's good to stick with the first name you pick and after the book is done decide if that name fits the story best. To change the name in the entire story just type:

FIND AND REPLACE

Jake with Prescott

Be careful not to pick names that may be cute and even beautiful but are also distracting. It is not easy to seduce your readers into taking a trip on your ship-of-words and keep them aboard.

Readers can be distracted by little things like air conditioner noises or distant train whistles. You want them to tune-out these real-world things and stay inside your story. So don't pick a name that makes them think – Hmm, the name Alacia rattles me a little.

Early in our book project we need to start a list of the main characters and some of the minor ones too. We are starting to write now so use the computer for later changes.

Here's one way to start defining characters but you don't need to fill in every line item:

Name	Tom
Sex - Age	M - 36
DOB	1963
Context	Jane's cousin
Description	Teeth too white ?

Disposition	Argumentative
Best trait	Educated
Worst trait	Know it all
Unique trait	Knows Egypt history cold

Some authors find it helpful to flip through a catalogue or a magazine to find photos that might be their Tom or Heather. I find my creative room offers more variety than photos do.

What is it about your main character that grabs your sight, smell, hearing or touch? Slumped posture, coffee breath, shrill voice, too fishy a handshake, aggressive, blinks too much.

Be diligent about noting anything that pops into your mind as your characters "talk" to you. For example:

Nick always steeples his fingers before he contradicts someone.

Lisa's eyebrows are pencil lines.

Why does Patrice drink her coffee through a straw?

How come Tom knows so much about old movies?

Why does Cindy insist on sitting in the back seat when we drive someplace?

Traits like this can be introduced early and "explained" later. Your reader wants to know too but don't explain it right away.

Maybe Nick's disciplinarian dad steepled HIS fingers when he chastised him.

Maybe Lisa had only one picture of her deceased mom - wearing the same eyebrows.

Maybe Patrice burned her lips bad a year ago when her pals hazed her in the college dorm.

Maybe Tom was a lonely projectionist at an all night movie house and he read the pile of old movie magazines while the film was running.

Maybe Cindy was in a terrible car crash as a child when she was four and her dad was high.

In real life, we all meet people who have unusual traits and find out much later what caused them. So when you introduce a "trait" early in your story and explain its "background" later,

>YOU ARE WRITING THE WAY LIFE IS.

That word "later" is important. Introducing a character trait and explaining it immediately is NOT as effective as letting it flow into the story later. Take care, however, to slip these explanations into the story stream without ripples.

Growth

For key characters to be interesting to your reader, they need to change during the story; not always for the better and not always in an extreme way. A guy that always tells the truth may tell a big lie at a critical plot point.

In *The Sky Tree*, after getting caught in the spider web, True Bee Kazo is not quite so reckless. The rabbit and beaver families are happier and, by story end, Minty changes a lot. Even Darrin gets "with it."

So when you're first inventing your players, think how they might "grow" from being "this" to "that." A "spacey" guy might save the day because he remembers the license plate number of the bad guy with the Red Sox hat.

Not everyone gets "gooder" though. Some trustworthy types may turn out to be real un-nice at a crucial time. Typically, the change in the hero or main character is for the better.

Your characters are more interesting if they have some unusual behavior pattern to begin with and more exciting when they "do the unexpected" later in your story.

Just remember, no change is boring.

Look what happens to a timid cowboy named Jake Brody who earlier saw a wolf mother save her pup when it fell into a river.

> Jake dashes along the shore and reaches for the newborn calf but he's too late. She slips on the rocky slime and flops headfirst into the swollen river. Honcho yells over the roar. "No way to save er JB. Forget it".

"Bullshit." Jake shouts back, "Not gonna have some wolf bitch be braver than me." He jumps in the white water and is sucked downstream as he struggles toward the frantic bawling.

Honcho watches them get washed around the bend.

The reader is delighted to see how Jake has responded. By the way, notice how this exchange did NOT happen. Here's how some start-up authors might write it.

"There is no way you can get to that calf, JB."
"Bullshit, "I am not going to have some wolf bitch be braver than I am.

Two cowboys on the trail do NOT talk that way nor do any other real people. When you write, your mission is NOT to show the reader you'd really like to be an English teacher.

When people are into a gut exchange, words like "going to" become "gonna". So while you're observing personalities, listen to how they really talk because capturing reality is now part of your job as an author.

First Appearance

At the first appearance of a character, I like to tag her or him with a Mini-ID before jumping in to a deeper description. This gives the reader an immediate "strap" to hang onto as the scene progresses. For example:

One Way To Write 65

The knock surprised Alex. Room service couldn't be that fast. Before he got the door opened all the way, he could smell a trace of baby powder. Been awhile since he last smelled that sweet aroma. He swung the door open and saw she was no baby.

She nodded, "Sorry to bother you at this hour. I'm Linda in room 504 above and I think my daughter may have dropped her sweater onto your balcony. Could we see if it's still there?"

Now as the two go take a look, you can blend in more impressions Alex might have about Linda but your reader already knows a tiny bit about her. She smells nice.

In *The Sky Tree*, we learn early that Darrin's tail has a brown tip. The reader visualizes that immediately. A writer can blend in more description later but at least the reader's imagination is already on board.

Before TV, radio listeners had to paint their own vibrant scenes with their imagination. In your story, a Mini-ID invites the reader's imagination to start painting right away while **you keep some action moving.** (Is the sweater there or not? Is this some kind of scam? Is Linda a threat? Alex knows the floor above is a restaurant with no windows that can be opened...so how does he handle the visit? These could be thoughts your reader might enjoy evaluating.)

The suspense of a "strange" visit should not be slowed down while we are told about Linda's hair color, beauty, age, dress.

Instead, we can give the reader an immediate Mini-ID strap and cover a description of her when Alex relates the visit to a friend who asks:

> "Alex, how old was this…Linda? Whad she look like? What was she wearing? Ever see her before? Anyplace?"

Dialogue exposition that lets the reader sneak-listen-in is more captivating than an **OPOV** nuts and bolts (telling) description of Linda.

When you create suspense, don't interrupt it with story housekeeping. Let the reader enjoy the thrill ride and do the housekeeping later…preferably with a dialogue exchange.

In *The Sky Tree*, the reader sees a map of Misty Valley even before the story begins and gets a Mini-ID of **place** immediately.

The reader starts thinking about things that might happen in the forest or on Angry Island with those Mangler Ants. Hmmm?

STEP 15
Navigating Your Story

At this point, we are using the green book to snare ideas as they pop up and using the computer to build our story, to edit it and later, to send it to our publisher.

Don't laugh.

Here are some navigating tips that will save you hours of managing your 30,000-plus words. Do not ignore these suggestions without trying them because you need to move easily all around in what you've written, what you plan to write and what you decide to change.

Without a simple navigating system you'll get discouraged, your writing will stop being fun and any hope of vivid creativity will evaporate.

You can create separate files for the front cover, for the ISBN page, for the Author's Note, for the dedication, for the acknowledgements, etc. but ...

you should write your story in one document as follows:

Back Cover – blurb

Brief List of Characters (Names only)

First List of Chapter Names (no numbers)

   This will be the table of contents

Second List of Chapter Names (no numbers)

   These will be for your written chapters

Do not put each chapter in a separate document because juggling multiple documents with changing versions and different sequences is worse than water torture.

From your headlines you should have a rough idea how your story is going to flow. Create a list of all the (known) chapter titles to form a Table of Contents list. You can add more later.

Copy this list and paste it after the Contents list. This Second List is where you write each chapter so you need to type CCC in front of each of these chapter titles and you are ready to write.

Now using your word processor, you can work on any chapter you want by typing:

FIND CCC

This lets you jump through all 35 chapter titles in seconds to double-check some detail, make a change or add a gem.

You don't number your chapters because you'll have to fix the numbers whenever you relocate, add or delete a chapter. With CCC at every chapter heading, you can re-order them easily later with a COPY and PASTE.

When your book is done and the chapters are in their final sequence, you can number your chapters and correct the table of contents list.

Because it's so easy to move to any chapter in your story, you are more eager to tune your story with better ideas.

And you can (and should) also easily SAVE your current story as Version A and try out a different plot in Version B.

Do not trash the earlier versions because you may make a big change in version F and later wish you stayed with the earlier version D. All writers never want to write a chapter from scratch all over again.

Now, with your (CCC) chapter headings in place, you can work on any chapter that fits the mood you're in when you start your writing session.

Next, we need to print out a copy of the character list and put it where we can see it easily (on the wall or desktop). When you're creating soaring prose you don't want to de-soar just to search for the name of the New York cabbie that was on page two and again on page 304. No wonder you forgot, his name was Rosmond.

If you put the list on the desktop screen, you can easily jump to it to add creative thoughts about the character as they pop up.

Here's another time saver. Lets say we are writing precious creative prose. We're in the moment and our characters are telling us their story. Suddenly an exceptional thought comes to mind that solves an earlier plot problem like - the bullet was made of ice.

Don't stop your creative train of thought. Instead, just type:

XXX Ice Bullet

Then get right back into your creative moment and keep writing.

Any time later, you can type FIND XXX and skip to every one of your exceptional thoughts without bashing any of your creative moments.

So if, for example, you need to look up how many legs the Mangler Ant should have, rather than rock your creativity boat trip just type XXX ant legs and keep writing your inspired words.

Later you can address all of the XXX items when you're creative gas tank is empty. Learning that ants have six legs takes no creative gas.

How about when in the middle of our inspiring prose, the FedEx guy rings the front door bell. Just type XXX, save your work and answer the door. How bout you're doing a rewrite at midnight and you're tired. Type RRR and the date, save your work and go to bed. Three days later you can jump right back to where you stopped your rewrite.

Here's another tip that saves time.

As soon as you have a table of contents, add WWW at the top of the list and four zeros off to the right of each item. Here a partial list for 1W2W:

WWW Work-to-be-done list.

Why Write	O
What To Write	O
The Green Book	O
Short Stories	O
Writers Workshops	O
Magazines etc	O O O O

Word Processor	O O O O
Field Trips	O O O O
When To Write	O O O O

The four zeros next to each chapter represent 100 percent of work that needs to be done. Here we see that drafts of the first four sections have been written but need a rewrite and the last four sections haven't yet been started.

Now we can zoom to:

WWW	Work done and still needs to be done
CCC	Any Chapter we want
XXX	Any exceptional idea or fix-up spot

You can see that even a simple 90 page children's book has a lot of information that has to be shuffled, researched and revised.

You may not need any of these housekeeping aides to preserve your creative moments but guys like me who are light on talent need all the help they can invent.

We can look up rules for grammar, punctuation, hyphenation, tense agreement and spelling but…

WE CAN'T LOOK UP CREATIVITY ANYWHERE.

To keep creativity our number one priority, we need to make all the other tasks as simple as possible.

Tomorrow, when you start to write with a fresh brain, work on what you haven't even started yet. Later when you're tired or only have an hour to fill, work on items like research, your XXX items or housekeeping things (chapter re-sequencing).

STEP 16
Fine Bone Skeleton

So by now, we've snuck up on a good story using a back cover, some headlines and a big bone skeleton. We can move around all our documents to maximize creativity. We can update our character list (and traits) as we write. We know that a sketch and map can help us think up scene details. We know how to connect our mood and energy level to our creative and housekeeping tasks. We know how to stay creative when interruptions, new ideas or plot problems pop up.

Next we use these tools to complete the story body with the fine bones so we can add conflict and drama that seems real.

Here is the big bone skeleton of Chapter 1 from *The Sky Tree:*

> Two bees wait in a Pine tree for the birth of a squirrel

That's it.

Now we need some finer bones:

> Two True Bees watch and wait for the birth
> Weeks earlier they had waited for two crows to hatch
> It's their job to spread any news throughout the forest
> A baby crow falls from her nest
> The bees argue about who should go get the dad crow
> They strike a deal

We're almost ready to flesh out the skeleton but who will tell the story?

The easiest way to write a story is to use the OPOV and the **past** tense. But to bring my reader into what's happening in *The Sky Tree*, I use the OPOV and the **present** tense.

Since readers feast on **dialogue**, I needed an **A** to talk to a **B** in the first scene of *The Sky Tree* so the reader could "listen in." A fantasy story can have talking animals, insects, birds and trees if we want it to so I had two bees talk to each other about what's happening.

After we think up our story line (back cover) and create headlines to see if the story hangs together, we need to build a big bone skeleton using a POV and tense. Then we can add some small bones for problems, conflicts and drama.

When you write your book, your hero needs to have a partner, or pal, or a friendly bartender so he or she can talk to someone (and let the reader listen in). Just having an OPOV TELL the story is usually not enticing for long.

Lets look at the first chapter of *The Sky Tree*. It would be all "tell, tell, tell" if I didn't have the bees do some "show-with-dialogue" what's going on.

> Halfway up the nearest Pine, a pair of True Bees waits for the birth of a baby squirrel. Their big eyes never blink and their see-through wings are still. They don't mind waiting because it is their job to spread the news when a baby is born. And they love their job.
>
> A few weeks earlier, Diaz and Kazo waited in the same tree for two baby crows to arrive. They watched the white eggs with dark spots for the first nip of an egg tooth. Then they buzzed through the forest to tell all the animals and trees about Chakra and Crawford.
>
> Diaz sees something move up in the crow's nest. She points her antenna and whispers, "Kazo, look at that Chakra. She's going to fall, for sure."
>
> Kazo flicks his antenna but doesn't need to move his head to see Chakra swaying on oversized feet and flapping fluff covered wings. "She should know better…Oh my, she's falling."
>
> Chakra falls, bumps off a small twig and summersaults onto a soft raspberry bush near the stream below. More frightened than hurt; she crawls under a clump of grass near the falls and stays quiet.
>
> "Quick, Kazo, go get her mom."

"You go. I'll wait for the new baby squirrel."

"No. You go and I'll let you do all the telling about the new baby."

"Okay, it's a deal." Off he buzzes.

In your first draft, concentrate on just getting your story line on "paper."

In your "final drafts", you will need to convert all of the "telling" into "showing-with-dialogue" even if you have to invent some "scene observers."

Do not start your final drafts (yes, there will be more than one), until after you read about the story spices described in the next section.

But first…as they say on TV, it's time to give yourself a reward.

Go to Staples, Office Depot or go on-line and order yourself some quality business cards with a neat icon that shows the new you:

> Pat Nelson, Writer
> Address
> email – Phone

The first reason for doing this is you deserve a treat for following *your* dream and the second reason is:

Your new business card lets you ask anyone, any question, anytime you want and be welcomed.

"Professor, I'm a writer and I'm working on a story about problem management." (hand him or her a card) "I was wondering how you handle a student that's disruptive in class."

You can approach a cop, an animal trainer and anyone else that might give you some insight on your story.

One of my earlier stories had several scenes in a "gentlemen's club" or topless bar. By introducing myself (with a business card) to the manager, I interviewed him for two hours…well, maybe more.

He was one of the best managers I ever talked with. I learned that (1) Many of his performers had a family and needed to help with the expenses. (2) The ladies pay him a fixed rent for their work shift and every hour they must dance on stage for four minutes. (3) The rest of the time they serve drinks to customers and dance close by for tips. But what most surprised me was (4) The city code prohibited any liquor sales so after paying an entrance fee, each patrons had to buy a minimum of one bottle of water every hour at $4.00.

One of my story characters was an older topless dancer who was no longer in great shape so I asked him how he managed that situation at his club. His response… "It's not for me to decide what customers like or don't like. If she is not being asked to lap dance enough to pay her rent, she'll know."

I never would have been able to interview this manager if I didn't have a business card when I introduced myself.

I've also interviewed a Greyhound bus dispatcher, vice squad cop, race car driver, doctor, stone mason and others.

People are thrilled to be asked about their expertise…how would you feel after your third successful book if an aspiring writer handed you a business card and said, "Hi Pat, I'm a new writer and I was wondering what makes your dialogue sound so real. Mine seems a little stilted. Any suggestions?"

Get the idea? Good. Now go get some business cards.

That's what a real author would do.

STEP 17
Voice and Point of View

Lets take a look at chapter four from *The Sky Tree.*

As she grows into a beautiful young lady, Minty runs, climbs and plays with her friends like every day is party day. She's real fast so all her friends want her on their team. When she plays hide and seek, she is hard to find, especially when she hides under the nice smelling mint leaves near the blueberries. They smell so special to her.

Many of the guy squirrels really like her but Minty wants to find someone who might also like her secret dream of visiting the Sky Tree and climbing into the clouds.

Maybe Darrin would understand. She likes to be around him. He has a beautiful tan coat and his furry tail has a dark brown tip that she really likes.

He's a little shy but she knows he's brave because one day when Diaz showed her a place near the creek that had lots of acorns on the ground he rescued her. She was gathering acorns when two mean squirrels tried to take them away from her.

Diaz flew away to tell Darrin and just as the bad guys were about to take all her acorns. Darrin arrived, puffed up his fur and tail and stepped between them. His big eyes glaring, he squeaked right in their faces. They turned away and ran up an Oak tree. Diaz flew off to tell all the trees and animals how brave Darrin had protected Minty.

The first two of these paragraphs use the OPOV but notice paragraph three:

Maybe Darrin would understand. She likes to be around him. He has a beautiful tan coat and his furry tail has a dark brown tip that she really likes. He's a little shy but..."

This text seems more like it is Minty's thought process, almost a First Person POV thought. Then we go back to OPOV.

Lets look at an earlier example:

The knock surprised Alex. Room service couldn't be that fast.

Before he got the door opened all the way, he could smell a trace of baby powder. Been awhile since he last smelled that sweet aroma. He swung the door open and saw she was no baby.

She nodded, "Sorry to bother you at this hour. I'm Linda in room 504 above and I think my daughter may have dropped her sweater onto your balcony. Could we see if it's still there?"

Look at the line,

"Been awhile since he last smelled that sweet aroma."

Again, it seems that this is what he's thinking.

"And it lied to him…" This is another thought of his and we believe it.

The OPOV could have written,

"Alex's first impression from the aroma did not match up with her looks."

Instead we used a "voice" that is more intimate and believable.

When you write your story, be ready to morph from OPOV telling into the character's head to share his or her thoughts as they happen. This "internal thought dialogue" or "voice" can make your reader your biggest fan because your reader feels privileged to be let in on private feelings.

STEP 18
Tell v Show

People are luckier than other forms of life because when people acquire some new thing, they can share the news by telling or showing others the new "something".

News is usually fun to give and fun to receive.

Lets say you and your school pal Joe have a summer job at a supermarket. You're both on a break in the back room. He's eating a sandwich over behind the freezer and you're done eating so you're fooling around juggling four apples. Suddenly, you succeed in juggling all four at once. You've been trying to do this for weeks so your excited and you want to share the excitement with your friend.

You can shout over to him, "Hey Joe, I did it. Four apples at once in the air." Or you can stroll over by him, get his attention and put all four apples into orbit.

Which of these two ways of delivering the news is the most exciting to him? And you too?

Or, let's say you're twelve. It snowed all night and you just built your first snowman. How do you share the news with your mom or dad? Write them a note and describe it? Run in the house and tell them about it…or beg them to come take a look?

If you want your readers to love your work you need to share the excitement of your story by showing them what happened not telling them.

But you can't **show** them your entire story, you have to **tell** some of it. Some scene settings HAVE to be described by telling.

So your options are:

> Plan A   Tell, tell, tell, **show**, tell, tell, tell
>
> or
>
> Plan B   Show, show, show, **tell,** show

Here's all tell:

> Mary had a little Lamb whose fleece was white as snow. And everywhere that Mary went, the lamb was sure to go.

Here's all show:

> "Hi, little Lamb. My, how white your fleece is. I sure hope you're going to follow me to school again today. You ready?"

"Baaaah.
"Okay, lets go."

In *The Sky Tree*, two bees carry the story along using **dialogue that shows what's happening.** Later trees talk and rabbits and birds and...the important point is character dialogue SHOWS what's happening most of the time.

Now, in your story, when a big, rusty iron bridge falls, it can't say, "Hey, I'm falling." But you could have two hikers convey the excitement.

"Hey Mike, that middle section's swinging. Got to be half mile at least. Those rivets popping? Let's get the hell out here."

Here's another example where dialogue is substituted for telling. It's a sweet story about a mother who is making a doll named Missy for her young daughter, Mandy.

First, the "Tell" version:

Mandy was excited as she watched her mother every day add a little here and a little there. It was such fun to see her doll come to life. Glue, cardboard, buttons, snaps, felt, stuffing, yarn, string and pom-poms were used to create little Missy. Her shoes were made from cardboard covered in felt.

Next, the "Show" version:

"Can we start now, Mom?"

"Okay, Mandy, go get the box and we can work on Missy. Don't forget the pom-poms."

Mandy dashes to the closet for the big box filled with glue, buttons and stuffing. A loud little voice from down the hall, "When will Missy be done?"

"Oh, Mandy, you ask me that everyday. Your Missy wants to be dressed nice so it takes time. How 'bout today we make her arms from the cloth you picked out yesterday?"

Silence. Then. "But she needs shoes, too. What can we…? Oh, I know. How 'bout cardboard. And we could cover them with this." She holds up the light brown felt. Her smile brightens the hall.

"Well, we can ask Missy if she likes them.

Mandy runs back with the box, "Oh, she already told me yesterday she likes them."

"Okay, Mandy, then that's what we'll use."

Hint:

Avoid using LY adverbs that **tell** your reader how to interpret your words. Use **"dashed"** instead of **"ran quickly"**. Look for all the LY adverbs because they **tell** you that you need to write so that NO adverb-telling is needed. More about adverbs later.

STEP 19
The Recipe

So here's the recipe for your first book:

1. Pick a story idea
2. Write a back cover that hooks
3. Create story headlines
4. Build a big bone plot skeleton
5. Create main characters and others
6. Add finer bones for conflict and drama
7. Write a rough draft which **tells** your story
8. **Get ready to rewrite the entire story using only dialogue (unless impossible) and the following story spices.**

This is easier than you think because if you know that dialogue is the best end-form for your story, you start using it more and more in your draft and your rewrite task gets smaller with every chapter.

Don't feel bad about rewriting because only super talents can juggle characters, plot, dialogue, conflict, drama and spices at the same time. They all have to rewrite just like you and me but at least now you know what to shoot for…**story development by dialogue.**

With every rewrite cycle, we authors get more eloquent because we now know that dialogue trumps narration.

And here's a surprise.

As you go through these steps, your story will seduce you because when you try, for example, to add conflict or drama, you will find the best way to express them is with who said what to whom and **you start writing dialogue.** Perfect. Keep writing it. Let the characters talk to you and write their own scene.

This seduction by the characters is why many established authors prefer NOT to use a story outline. They know the most powerful way to convey a compelling story is to let the characters speak the story and let it roam in a way that soars over any outline.

We start-up authors need a plan for our first few books because we're skill learning while writing. This recipe can make your first book good and your second book great because by then you'll know how to create a captivating melody-harmony that needs little tuning.

And if you did pick a children's story for your first book and only one child likes it, isn't that more than enough reason to write it?

Me thinks yes.

STEP 20
Story Spices

Before you start any rewriting, you need to learn about these story spices:

Glue - Payoff – Tense - Verbs - Adverbs – Attribution - Exposition – Plot Shape – Pace – Spacing – Bill-boarding - Style – Tibs - Illustrations - Opening – Acid Test

As with any spice, YOU have to decide…how much to use.

Spice 1   Glue

As your characters live out their story, they show up in different scenes, places and times. When your story time-line needs to be interrupted with flashbacks of background information you need to bring your reader over these "road bumps" in a way that does not jolt the reader's buy-in.

Most of the time, one scene leads naturally into the next. Here are the last lines of chapter four and the first of chapter five of *The Sky Tree*.

> Mom smiles, "We both will miss you a lot, Minty, but dreams are rare and need to be followed."
>
> Early the next morning, Minty is up before the sun...

The reader doesn't have to think about time or place and reads on. More dramatic changes in time and place can be handled with place headlines. Lets look at an example.

> OVAL OFFICE
>
> "Yes, Mr. President, I'll call the ambassador right away."
>
> LONDON, ENGLAND
>
> At dinner, Huxley Judd had just proposed a toast to Sir Walton Dale when the butler approaches and whispers, "Sir, Washington."

Here, the reader is guided over a big change in place in a way that flows with continuity.

"Story Glue" is used to blend changes in your story's place, time or subject in a way that is smooth, natural and enriching. It also is used to add needed information. For example, the hero cop talks to a buddy regularly (and informs the reader at the same time) about what's happening..

In *The Sky Tree*, Minty talks to Darrin and informs the reader about what's going on and what they are thinking. The True Bee's conversation help tie scenes together. The Wrinkly trees help tie chapters together. Darrin's grooming pops up from time to time. Sneak-climbing skill plays a big role near the ant camp where it becomes sneak-swim.

An event or characteristic introduced early in your story and later used in an important happening is a powerful form of story glue. Lots of small doses of glue work better than a few big globs. Take for example, the brown spot on Darrin's tail first mentioned in Chapter Three.

He doesn't like it. Minty does like it. In the cave, he wonders if she really likes it and later it gets nipped off by a Mangler Ant. Those are little bits of story glue.

Or…She likes Mint leaves, the Wrinkly surprises her with some in the cave and later the mint aroma almost dooms the two dreamers when a Mangler ant catches its aroma..

A map is also a great form of story glue because the reader can take small or large bites of information as needed and see where Angry Island is and where the party at Left Turn bend takes place.

Think, glue is good.

Spice 2   Payoff

"Payoff" and "Glue" are similar in that they both rely on an early intro and later use. Comedians call this the setup and payoff.

In *The Sky Tree* Darrin's habit of grooming pays off when his skill helps him free Blinky from the spider web. Maybe, in your book, having a character be an expert on rare postage stamps or the symptoms of strangulation or counterfeit money could help advance your plot.

Such expertise needs to be introduced early in your story in a natural way…his father collected stamps, her uncle was a pathologist, he worked for a mob-connected printer. Then, ten chapters later, it seems believable when that skill gets to help the hero.

Here's another form of story glue or payoff.

Your hero is a cop named Caniff. He and his partner Zabel are having a few beers after work. They're sitting in a back booth chatting about the case they're working on (exposition). Zabel visits the men's room and on the way back, he notices there's a dollar bill on the floor. He points to it. Caniff looks at it and shrugs. Zabel picks it up, pockets it and says,

"You saw that a'ready?"

Caniff nods and sips. Purses lips tight.

"How come you…?"

"Look Zay, it's bad luck. Last time I picked up dollar off the floor…"takes a sip…"within minutes, I was in an ambulance. S'long story an don want to talk about it."

Is this is a setup for a payoff later, maybe? Or is it glue because he's always spotting a coin and ignoring it. Or maybe in a late scene, a coin rolls across the floor at a critical moment.

This is the kind of stuff that lives in our creative room. Yes, we need to use skills of story telling and the seduction of style and the blending of spices but above all we need to tap into that rich source of ideas that lives in our head.

Your creative genie is the toughest giant to set free.

But you have to try.

Spice 3   Tense

The past tense is easy to use and easy to read so most fiction authors use it.

> Miller tried to take careful aim but his hand
> trembled from being smashed by the shovel.
> He switched hands and fired.

The present tense is not quite as easy to use but it brings a sense of NOW to your story.

Miller tries to take careful aim but his hand
trembles from being smashed by the shovel.
He switches hands and fires.

Which of these versions bring you into the scene best?

The easiest way to get your story on paper is to use the past tense and THEN decide if certain scenes would work better in the present tense. It is not hard to change tense after you have a first draft. You will need to refine many scenes to add spice elements anyway so pick a scene and try both the past and present tenses to decide what works best.

The present tense brings the reader into the scene and close to the action, close to the thoughts and the dialogue but blending in (past) background information can jolt the reader a little as the writer switches tense.

Present
Both dogs chase after the rolling meatball. Skipper has no chance.
Mandrake had six brothers so all his meals were races.
Past
Both dogs chased after the rolling meatball. Skipper had no chance.
Mandrake had six brothers so all his meals were races.

The past tense is natural to way for your reader to "hear" the story AND "hear" the background information in one smooth flow.

A simple test for all this is for you to write a scene from The Three Bears or The Three Little Pigs in the past tense and then in the present tense. Your gut feel will tell you which tense to use for your first book. If in doubt, use the past tense...and save the present tense for your next book.

Spice 4   Verbs – Active vs. Passive

Active	Tom ate all the vanilla ice cream
Passive	All the vanilla ice cream was eaten by Tom.

Now this is where I need to ask for your help. If you know of any good reason why the passive presentation should ever be used, please share it with me because I can't think of any. Sometimes it fills a need (I'm told) but you should pretend a passive verb costs you twenty dollars whenever you use one.

Spice 5   Adverbs

Very, loudly, sadly

Let me tell you about Pa Brown. He was my English teacher in Weymouth high school. A strict disciplinarian and demanding instructor. On the first day of our class he let us know his rules. The killer was:

If you use "VERY" in your essays, you get an F on your paper.

Wow, what was that all about? But over the months it dawned on all of us. If you can't use VERY you have to think of an alternative so your thinking improves, your vocabulary improves and your writing improves.

Pa Brown, I love you.

As for you, the reader of 1W2W, never use the word VERY. Pa Brown will be upset and you will be admitting your thinking, your vocabulary and your writing is very lazy.

Oops.

Do not upset Pa Brown.

In the world of fictional writing, Adverbs should be called Aspirin because they are often used when the writing is not (done) well – especially the adverbs ending in -ly. happily, sadly. Every time you use some adverbs you are **telling** your reader how to interpret what your character is saying or how he's feeling or how he's acting. You are doing this because your writing is not expressive enough to convey the mood of the scene without an ly-adverb.

Yes, some adverbs seem to be *the* perfect word for a phrase.
    Tom was upset but Joe was even *more* upset.
But even this phrase could be punched up:
    Tom was upset but Joe was shocked and speechless.

Lets look at two ly-adverb examples:

Version A

<u>Quickly</u> Patrice turned to him and said <u>sadly</u>, "That really surprises me, Robert, I expected you'd have the guts to tell him you wouldn't lie for him."

Version B

Patrice snapped around to be sure he wasn't joking but her eyes teared up because she knew. A whisper, "That surprises me, Robert…" She shook her head…" I expected you'd have the…the guts to tell him you wouldn't lie for him."

Story tellers use ly-adverbs to **tell** their readers what to think.

Story authors use happenings, reactions and dialogue so their readers can "see, hear and decide for themselves" what to think.

Version B uses twice the words version A does. So it's tempting to write Version A stuff because it's *more* efficient. Adverbs may be okay for a preliminary draft but if you are always telling your readers what the character's words mean instead of inviting their emotions to participate they will wonder why they are always being told what to think.

Who likes that?

Not kids. And not grown-ups.

The Rx is…consider every adverb to be a flag for a richer expression.

I'm sure I use some in *The Sky Tree*. When you have a spare moment, why not count how many I use in the 20,000 words. Could my story have been written better? Of course.

But hey, my first book. Jeez.

Spice 6   Attribution - He asked, she said.

All of us are well trained to "tune out" the packages that art comes in.

We watch a TV show about a man surviving in the wild and rarely wonder who is shooting the video. We see the movie, "The Birds" and never hear the music.

And we read captivating dialogue and never notice, "he said or she said."

Be alert. You can add <u>vivid color</u> to your story by replacing attributions like "he said or she asked" with color-tags. Lets take a look at the difference.

Attributions:

>"Who told you that?" he asked.
>"Get outa here." she said. "That never happened. You want to publish this stuff, you're on your own."

Color Tags:

> He glared, "Who told you that?"
> She punched his arm, "Get outa here. That never happened."
> He slammed the book on the table. "You want to publish this stuff, you're on your own."

Color tags replace bland housekeeping furniture with dramatic imagery. We don't need furniture in our story, we need color.

And how about using: glared, punched, slammed, snapped instead of asked and said. You can punch up your writing by NEVER using an attribution. Just have the character do some tiny action before he or she speaks.

In *The Sky Tree*, the word "said" is used three times.

Once you let your reader know who makes the first comment, you do not need ANY attribution OR any color-tag if it is obvious from the exchange who is doing the talking. To deepen the emotion as the exchange gets heated, use a color tag.

If more than two people get talking you can ID the new speaker with a color tag then get out of your reader's way as he or she gets hooked on your scene.

Spice 7   Exposition

Exposition is the sharing of background information the reader needs to know to appreciate your story's full dimension.

Many stage plays open with a living room scene where the phone rings and "Roger" answers it. "Hello. Oh hi, Linda, I was just - (long pause) Was Tom hurt bad? (pause) Yeah, sure."

Roger's wife Susan enters, looks concerned.

Roger holds up his hand for silence. "Okay we'll come right away." Roger hangs up. Susan is wringing her hands. Roger turns to her. "Your brother, another DUI."

We learn through dialogue exposition that Susan's brother, Tom, is (probably) a habitual drunk and he's (probably) in some hospital.

This often-used exposition device is known as "the maid's phone call." Many TV shows use a phone call for exposition or a TV news channel in the background to deliver context for the story. Maybe we get to see an accused mobster interviewed so we "believe" the bad stuff he does later.

You will need to create exposition for your story also. Try to **deliver it in small bites** and use dialogue if possible. Notice the phone call above was all dialogue.

Raw exposition can come across like a history book.

Don't start a chapter or a scene with exposition. Start with dialogue or action to hook your readers first then slip in exposition in small hunks. A little history goes a long way.

Sure we need to know history to appreciate today, but not all at once. And not by being told. We prefer to "overhear" A talking to B about what happened before.

Next time you watch a sit-com, pay close attention to the early scenes to see how script writers deliver exposition on who the players are and what the problems are.

Some of it is poorly done.

"Angel! You mean Larry, your brother, shot the guy?"

Like Angel doesn't remember that Larry is her brother!

It's fun to watch these opening scenes as three or four people walk along and bring each other (and the viewer) up to date on what's happening. We (almost) don't notice the simple exposition because it's so much fun to "eavesdrop" on the dialogue.

That alone should convince you that even a bad story using dialogue is more captivating than a good story using tell-tell-tell. If you can think up a good story, it will be great if you share it using dialogue.

Look at how many exposition words the map in *The Sky Tree* saves the reader? And the *reader* gets to decide how long he or she wants to study it; a brief glance or a long moment to feed imagination with more visits later after reading about the entrances to the Spider-web subway. And a map *shows* the reader the needed info instead of *telling* the reader about it.

Read chapter one of *The Sky Tree* or any other book and highlight the exposition. Is it delivered by dialogue or by telling? Is it graceful, boring, natural or too long? Does it slow the "action?"

If you need a long exposition section, try breaking it up with a question or an action by a character.

Let's say your Detective Caniff needs to fill in his partner by cell phone. If your exposition needs to run long because it's complex, you could have Caniff hit a cell phone dead zone and get so ticked he almost crashes his car. We can "paint" the Caniff character by showing his temper and what he does. Then we can continue the needed exposition when, calmer, he calls from a "live" cell phone zone and continues to fill in his partner (and the reader).

And we can make this into story glue. We can have Caniff run in to cell-dead-zones a lot. Maybe at a critical plot point where he has to make a call to the cavalry. The bad guys are closing in and he needs backup. He reaches for his cell phone. Guess what? You tell me.

So here we can take dull story furniture (exposition) and shape it into tension bits or character painting.

Spice 8   Plot Shape

We go to writing school every day and don't even think about it. When we watch a TV drama, we can almost smell when a commercial break is about to happen because the story is at some climatic point. TV scripts are shaped and timed to carry viewers over the commercial breaks.

We need to shape our plots with problems of increasing severity until the (protagonist) hero finally overwhelms all of the problems and achieves her or his goal.

Earlier, we learned how conflict and drama enrich the plot that we started with our back-cover idea. As you review your story's draped skeleton, try to have the hero almost win the day only to be set back somehow. The reader wants her or him to try again so a "failure" at the end of a chapter helps you create a page-turner story.

Then to tease the reader's interest, switch to a different character for the next chapter. Leaving your readers to wonder helps bring them deeper into your story.

The hero's problems should be first just a nuisance, then big, then bigger, then huge and then impossible. Think of Minty, the tree is far away, she needs a pal, she needs permission, she is delayed by the thorny bushes, the ants are bigger than she expected, they sneak-swim and are almost snagged by the Mangler ants. But they reach their goal. Lets hope the reader is pulling for them all the way.

Look at the headlines of your story. You might want to shuffle their sequence to make your plot profile big, bigger, biggest. Just before your hero wins the day, it is good theater to have it look like all is lost.

Spice 9   Pace

Suppose: You're the coach of the Trenton High School Tigers and the big football game is tomorrow. You hold a run-through practice to hype the energy of the team. What music do you play over the speaker system? Rock n Roll or Easy Listening?

New suppose: Your hero is the best man for his brother's wedding but he's late and has to race across town to make it on time. What music is playing on his speakers as he speeds through traffic. Rock n Roll or Easy Listening?

You don't get to play background music in your book. Instead you get to use short snappy sentences or long beautiful sentences. Your dialogue can be crisp and sharp or poignant and tender. What length sentences best capture a chase scene? A seduction scene? A combination of both adds interest but the "action" dictates which length is most effective.

When your Judy has to explain to her young daughter that her pet hamster has expired your writing needs to come right out of your gut. Let it decide short or long and you "stay out of it."

But when your hero is racing to the hospital with a replacement heart in the cooler, you need to "punch up" the action with snappy words and short sentences.

Spice 10   Spacing

Compare the following two version:

- - - Version A - - -

Ten minutes later, Darrin finishes his grooming, walks quietly into the cave and lies down. He sees Minty over in a far corner. He takes a deep breath and settles into the grass. He's dead tired from the trip. His eyes close for a second then he whispers, "You really like my brown tipped tail, Minty?"
"Minty?"
"Ah, she's conked out. Well, it is a pretty distinctive shade." His smile fades and his mouth opens as he falls asleep.

- - - Version B - - -

Ten minutes later, Darrin finishes his grooming, walks quietly into the cave and lies down. He sees Minty over in a far corner.

He takes a deep breath and settles into the grass. He's dead tired from the trip. His eyes close for a second then he whispers, "You really like my brown tipped tail, Minty?"

"Minty?"
"Ah, she's conked out. Well, it is a pretty distinctive shade."
His smile fades and his mouth opens as he falls asleep.

Which version is more inviting to you? Which version captures the moment best?

Now ask a friend to read both versions and answer the same two questions. The impressions of you and your friend should help shape how you SPACE the words, lines and paragraphs of your book.

When readers see your words, they see the spacing also. Spacing invites your reader's emotions to get involved.

Spacing can also convey a tender moment or, at the end of a chapter, create reader anticipation.

Here's the end of Chapter 3 from *The Sky Tree*

> But from then on, that's all Minty could think about. She waits for windy days so she can see the Sky Tree again. At night, she dreams that one day she will travel to those hills, offer Sky Tree some water and ask it if she can climb into the clouds.
>
> Minty has a secret dream.

Spice 11   Bill-boarding

You turn on your TV and hear an anchor say,

> "Landslide blocks off the coast highway. Local man finds $10,000 in dumpster. Film at eleven."

The broadcast lingo for this is, "a tease or bill-boarding the news." It's effective at holding viewer interest while a commercial is run.

A tease at the end of a chapter is effective at keeping your reader plugged into your story. Example:

> Detective Stevens punches off his cell phone, nods at the tattooed kid and sighs, "Okay, Mango, Records tell me you were in jail when she was shot. Any idea who mighta done it?"
>
> Mango sniffs like his nose itches but he's cuffed so he just wiggles it. "Naw. Nobody I know woulda used a .22. You kidding? Guys I know would used sumpin bigger. Must'a been somun from that gang on Carlson. Still learning how, I guess."
>
> Steven gets close up, Real close. Whispers,"Well just the same, Mango, you lemmie know if ya hear any buzz on the street. Got no problem owing ya one later on. Right?"
>
> A shrug and head bob. Mango turns around. Stevens unlocks the cuffs, "Good to go, Mango."
>
> "Aw right. If I hear, ya know?" Mango's pants almost fall all the way off. Another nod and he swaggers away.
>
> Stevens shakes his head. No one else knows what caliber killed her.
>
> How come Mango knows?

In the next chapter you can continue the Stevens-Mango story line or jump to a new character and new story line knowing that your reader ALSO wants to find out…

> How come Mango knows?

Notice that the spacing of the last line helps build its impact. It could have been written:

> Stevens shook his head. No one else knew what caliber killed her. How come Mango knows?

But this version has less impact.

Spice 12   Style

Our style leaves our fingerprints all over our story because it reflects how we observe, listen, think and then how we convey events, personalities and emotions.

We write best when we are alone and become at one with our characters. We look around our scene to see what's happening. Is our character happy, sad, angry, determined, threatened, surprised or confused? These thoughts tug emotions out of our brain and send them through our fingers to the keyboard.

Our best writing happens when we stay in the character, in the scene and in the drama to capture the "moment". THAT'S also what captures our readers.

You will know when you're in the moment when you glance at the time and are shocked to see that it is four hours later than you thought it was.

This moment is also what will make you WANT to get up at 4 a.m. and write your next scene…and your next book. This moment is what confirms you are now an author.

Lets look at why capturing the moment is so essential.

Suppose we see a great movie called Payday. It's about a bank robbery that turns into a hostage drama. We see everything that happens and hear all of the dialogue. The suspense is spellbinding so we recommend Payday to our friends and they also think it's a great movie.

What just happened? Well, to begin with – if a picture is worth a thousand words, we just got six million video words and seventy thousand audio words and sound effects and music and we never noticed it was a three-hour film. Not bad.

We also didn't notice the virtual story elements like the somber music when bad things were about to happen or the collage of twenty-five jump cuts showing the cops getting weapons, cruisers speeding to the scene, yellow tape blocking off the crime scene, the bull horn getting grabbed – all this with snappy music. No wonder Payday was so great.

For authors, this presents some good news and some bad news.

The bad news is we writers need to figure out how to convey the 6,070,000 "words" of Payday onto 300 pages to make our book great. Good luck.

The good news is our style can make our book greater than great.

Before we see how, I need to remind you that eloquent style is not as essential in a children's story as it is in an adult book. Your children's story can be light and breezy, funny, and whimsical. True, these are elements of style but not the kind needed for a compelling, dramatic, mature novel that leaps off the bookstore shelf.

Now that we have a feel for blending basic writing skills into a delicious book-meal, we can look at your first fiction where style is THE most important skill to master.

First, try to paint the scene using <u>dialogue</u> as much as possible because it delivers realistic believability. Next, if dialogue won't play, use the character's <u>internal dialogue</u> (thoughts). And last, let the <u>POV tell</u> the story.

An author's work is most memorable when moving gracefully among:

    A Spoken dialogue (first choice)

    B Internal thought "dialogue" (next choice)

    C Telling (last choice)

This skill is only learned by writing but, once it is learned, your characters speak naturally, share their thoughts easily, your fiction writes itself and your reader gets locked into your drama and conflict.

Here's an example of moving through A, B and C:

> C- The knock surprised Alex. B- Room service couldn't be that fast.
> C- Before he got the door opened all the way, he could smell a trace of baby powder.
> B- Been awhile since he last smelled that sweet aroma.
> C- He swung the door open and saw she was no baby.
> C- She nodded,
> A- "Sorry to bother you at this hour. I'm Linda in room 504 above and I think my daughter may have dropped her sweater onto your balcony. Could we see if it's still there?"

Lets look again at:

> Been awhile since he last smelled that sweet aroma.

Is this line "telling" or is it a "thought-dialogue"? It's a close call. I say it's closer to a thought-dialogue than a tell.

It could have been written,

> "Alex thought, 'Been awhile since last I smelled that sweet aroma."

That would be telling and the OPOV-Tell is less intimate.

By now you can see that moving around gracefully in A, B and C is not easy but since dialogue is THE most important device for creating believability, it's an important skill for you to focus on.

Lets look at our earlier example for:

A- Spoken dialogue

B- Internal thought "dialogue"

C- Telling

C- Officer Ken Mason likes the thick hedge near the stop sign. B- Late-for-work drivers rarely look to the right. C- The chest high hedge hides his motorcycle but not his view. Mason just sits back on the saddle and folds his arms. B- He's careful not to touch the sharp creases of his blue uniform. He knows by noon, he'll be wishing he'd worn his tans.

B- Right now his only challenge is to decide when is a stop really a stop and not a slow glide through the intersection.

C- Over the hedge he sees a yellow Honda B- A customer, maybe? Nope. C- Honda boy actually stops then heads up Broadway. Ken watches him pass. B- Kid must be barely twenty. B- Music blaring.

B- Quiet again. Best part of his day is the morning briefing. Cop humor is so twisted. Especially, Romero's stuff. C- Ken is smiling as a red Mustang rolls through the stop and, with a short tire squeak, heads up Broadway

C- He punches the starter, gets a purr and thinks Lady Customer, here I come.

He lights up the red spots and rolls after her.

She doesn't pull over right away and his amusement morphs into annoyance. He's sure she sees the spots. The Mustang slows to a stop, motor on. He brakes, touches down his boot heel and kicks out the stand. Kills the motor. Blue Red flashers still on.

C- Studied calm movement as he approaches. A- "Morning, Miss. Could I see your license and registration, please."

C- A nod and half smile, A- "Officer, you happen to know Lieutenant Cooper?"

The A, B, C style choice is: When you can't use dialogue, use thoughts (internal dialogue). Just write the thought without introducing it with, Ken thinks, "etc." And when you can't use either A or B, use C, telling.

Even film-makers, with all of their enormous visual and audio power, use flashbacks with earlier dialogue and/or the character's voice-over thought-process to capture and carry viewers. That's how valuable dialogue is to believability.

Dialogue is so important, we need to study it in depth.

We all carry the baggage of our background with us. The older we are the more baggage we have. We pick up dialects, expressions, habits and mannerisms of those we associate with. The power of the English language comes from its adaptability. I believe fiction should be written in today's idiom. We should write the way people talk if we want our writing to capture our readers.

Few people are aware of what everyday dialogue is really like.

When Dad decides to go to the supermarket, he doesn't say, "I am going to the store. Do you need anything?" He says, "Goin to the store. Need anything?"

Try leaving out the pronouns I, we, you, they and see if your dialogue doesn't seem more real.

And here's yet another way people really talk. I call this NR, the non-response. Dialogue sounds more realistic when your character A speaks and character B's response does NOT seem to link with what A just said.

Here's how it flows.

> Ziggy is a bartender at the Cool Club. He's a likable guy but has a gambling problem and owes his bookie, Sam, $15,000. Sam tells his muscle guy, Oleg, to pay Ziggy a visit and talk to him.
>
> A half hour before closing time, Oleg drops in and takes a seat at the far end of the bar, away from the TV set and the two remaining customers. Ziggy rinses the last of four glasses, strolls over to Oleg, puts a coaster on the bar. He's smiling but his hand trembles.

> "Evenin, what can I get you?"
> "What's your friend usually want?"
> "My friend?"
> "You know Sam?"
> "Hey, I'm good for...next week for sure, I just need..."
> "Milk."
> "Scuze me?"
> "Milk. Can I get a glass of milk?"
> Ziggy eyes dart as he hurries back to the undercounter fridge. Please God, is there any milk left?

Next time you listen to casual conversation, concentrate on how normal dialogue does NOT connect. When A asks a question or makes a comment, the response by B *seems unconnected.*

Here is an example of a normal, believable exchange:

> "Going to the drug store. Need anything."
> "Johnny has to be at soccer by ten."
> "Can't Brent's mom take him?"
> "English muffins, we may be out. Check an see."

Yes, you need to unlock creativity to capture readers and keep them but you also have to listen to and absorb how people really talk with each other...what they say and what they don't say... so you can write it in a believable way.

Style also includes being open to adaptability. Today, the young generation is moving as fast as the technology they embrace.

Not everyone shakes hands the old way. Young people bump knuckles, hug or high five. Innovation is here to stay. It's okay to end a sentence with a preposition because that's the way we talk. Many say between you and me. Big deal. The purpose of style is not to show how much grammar you know. It's to yank your readers so solidly into your scene they think they're intruding.

And you can only do that if you capture the idiom of NOW.

One last word about style. If you learn to translate your observations and listening into faithful expressions of how life really happens, one day you may write a scene where a baby seal named Princess is trapped beneath the ice and looking for her breathing hole. Will she make it or not? When your tears fall onto your keyboard… you will know that you've captured every nuance of that happening.

Spice 13   Tibs - Tiny Information Bits

We all like to learn something we didn't know. A tiny bit of new information is a gift we appreciate receiving and feel a little smarter when we examine it. If few other people know of "the bit" we feel we're on the inside of something. I call these Tiny Information Bits "Tibs" and here's how they help your story.

Lets say you are writing about a bad cop in the 1930's who has a habit of skimming drugs or cash from street dealers. Years ago, he was involved in a shooting. Internal Affairs found it was a bad shoot and he almost lost his job. From then on, he carried a throw-down.

A throw-down is a second untraceable weapon that can be "tossed down" in a bad shooting. "The guy reached for a gun." Throw downs are not used these days. Readers find this kind of Tib is fascinating.

From the Tibs in *The Sky Tree* we learn there are over 300 kinds of squirrels. Some live in the ground and some in trees. Ants can carry twenty times their weight. Stalactites form overhead. Male squirrels groom more than female squirrels. Readers like these tiny information gifts if they are blended in your story in a natural weave.

Examples of Tibs might be:

> How do players cheat at roulette?
>
> Why don't woodpeckers get headaches?
>
> How is paper for currency made?

Spice 14   Illustrations

If you elect to write a children's story for your first book, you will probably need illustrations.

My grandchildren (6 and 8) already read well. I wrote *The Sky Tree* for kids (7 to 13) to read and for parents and grandparents to read to them. So the target age is fuzzy. Fantasy appeals to older readers too. Think Harry Potter.

Since I like to draw, I did my own illustrations for *The Sky Tree*. When you visit the bookstore to look for models of your first project, you will see that many children's books have drawings that look like first-graders did them. If your first project is a children's book I'm sure you could also do your own drawings or have a young person draw some.

Many classroom teachers would love such a project for their students. Find a teacher and ask her or him. Get creative. Visit a senior painting class and ask them to do some sketches. There are lots of starving art folks that will gladly give you a low quote to get published and the Internet is a great place to start looking for them.

Do not let some simple drawings stop your book. Writing is way too enjoyable to give it up.

Spice 15   Opening

Question   What never happens?

Answer   A second chance at a first impression.

That's why most book covers are in color.

But the next impressions are important too like the back cover synopsis, the author's bio, the table of contents, the first few pages

One Way To Write

and a map even. The first few lines of your story are also part of the "first" impression. Some browsers flip pages for illustrations, figures and tables.

While these impressions cascade onto the browsers, they "try on" the book they're holding to see if it fits their mood. "Do I want a mystery today? Or a thriller? A sweet story for Tessa? Or a dragon story for Bauer?

Your story's opening few lines should *expand* on the other first impressions of your book in a way that embraces rather than jolts. This keeps the browser on your side.

Pretend you're browsing *The Sky Tree* or some other book. Check out the front cover, back cover, first few pages, the map and the first few lines of Chapter One. Does the opening expand on the other first impressions of the book? Browsers who join a story at the cover need to be seduced by each next step of their exploring right up to and including your opening lines.

And dialogue is THE most seductive device you can offer. Start using it early and often.

In *The Sky Tree,* I could have opened with,

"Kazo, look at that Chakra. She's going to fall for sure."

While captivating, this opening does not expand and embrace the impressions already absorbed by *The Sky Tree* browser. But this jolt opening would be great for an action story. Dialogue AND action!

Look at your front cover, back cover, contents and decide how your opening **can embrace** what's already shaped a browser's first impression.

Hint 1: If you decide to open with calm expansion, be sure to get into some action early. In *The Sky Tree*, the calm opening is followed by a "jolt" when Chakra falls from her nest.

Hint 2: If you decide to open with a jolt, be sure to get into some calming happenings early.

In an opening, having one "mood" followed by its opposite validates both moods because life is NOT all jolt or all calm. So your writing is lifelike.

Spice 16   Acid Test

After a few rewrites of your manuscript, you will consider it ready for sharing.

Don't share it.

Put it away for ten days and forget everything about it. On day eleven, go off by yourself and read it out loud like you were recording a tape. Recording it is not a bad idea. If you don't think so, later try one chapter and then decide. But first, just read it out loud.

Don't forget our pledge. We don't share our work-in-process with anyone.

During this out loud reading you will get curious new feelings about how your story sounds. Circle these spots for later fixing and keep reading. The ten day wait sharpens your sensitivity to awkward passages. You will find dialogue that is great and dialogue that is "way off target." If you have used illustrations, are they in the right place?

After you make changes. Read it out loud again.

And don't forget…Pa Brown is listening for those sneaky adverbs.

STEP 21
Editing and Rewriting

I recommend you do your own **editing** for your first book but before you start, you need to be convinced that your **rewriting** is pretty much done because it's hard to combine editing with story changing without doing one or both poorly.

So look at every chapter and scene to be sure you have covered place and time, moved into the action early and didn't linger too long near the close. Does every scene have a balanced start, middle and end? Not too much of any one?

Short sentences should outnumber long sentences. Break up the long ones.

Look at every character's first appearance to be sure you have defined them for the reader's initial visualization with a Mini-ID, then added more later if it was needed.

Look at exposition sections for smooth entry, exit and short duration. Especially look for exposition passages that could be conveyed with dialogue instead of a history or back-story.

Look at dull verbs to see if they could be punched up with snappier alternatives.

Look for adverbs ending in "-ly." Find a way to save the $10 they cost you and use a crisp color tag if possible.

Look for passive verb phrases to see if an active version can add punch gracefully.

The charges for an editing service run from $250 and up for a 20,000 word story. Your hired editor may *not* realize your style includes slang and words like "gonna". The editor knows the rules for a term paper and a thesis but a story style is less predictable so the advice may be less valuable for your first book.

Doing your own editing and proof-reading also gives you yet another look at your work from a different viewpoint, a technical one.

Ask a friend to edit one or two chapters. The number of markups will show you what your next best step should be.

STEP 22
Proofreading

For your first book, I recommend you do your own proofreading. Start with your computer's spell-checker even if you are a good speller because it spots duplicate words back to back. He went **to to** the store.

You can find proofreading services on the Internet.

Lets assume you have produced a short story with:

    20,000 words

    250 words per page

    80 pages

If you Google "Proofreading" you will find that many companies provide hints to help you do your own proofing. That may be all you need.

Proofreading charges for a 20,000 word story also run from $250 up depending on how fast you want your work returned.

Typically, you e-ship your story to this service in a PDF-file or WORD-file and, when your story is returned, you can make or ignore any changes recommended.

Before you sign up for any of these services, give the story to friends and ask them to circle any errors or confusion spots. Better still, give your story to a non-friend and ask him or her to mark it up. You'll get more savage comments but it's up to you to evaluate them for merit.

STEP 23
ISBN – International Standard Book Number

Your work product is automatically copyright protected when you create your book. Some authors also register their work product but that offers little, if any, additional protection.

You will need an ISBN to get your book published but first you need decide if you will be writing a second and third book.

An excellent source for guiding you through this process is:

The Step-By-Step-Guide to Self-Publishing for Profit!

By C. Pinero and Nick Russell

This reference covers the trade-offs of becoming your own publisher or using an existing publisher. In either case, you will need an ISBN number for your book. Publishers can sell you one of their ISBN's for about $25 or you can buy ISBN's directly from Bower, the authorized distributor.

I bought my own block of ten ISBN's ($250) because I am writing more books and want to be my own publisher. The owner of the ISBN is the owner of the book and controls all rights unless contracted otherwise.

Publishers offer different plans for handling printing, order taking, shipping, administrating expenses and royalties. Their expertise is worth their fee and lets you concentrate on your next book.

STEP 24
Mock-Up

About now, you start thinking about what your book is going to look like. Hard or soft cover? Trim size? Font type and size? Color? These selections will affect your production costs.

Your book can be any size you want but publishers usually have standard "trim sizes" to keep production costs low. Many fine books now use a soft cover (in color) and, to keep the cost low, internal black and white illustrations.

If you decide to include illustrations, tables, diagrams or figures in your book, I suggest you create a hard copy mock-up using the font size(s) you want used and margin settings that fit the trim size you selected then mark where and how you want your graphic placed.

You should at least make a mock-up of the pages where graphic placement is critical.

Your e-publisher sends you an e-form so you can define where the graphics go but a mock-up helps convey any special treatment when graphics and text are side-by side or text is wrapped.

No mock-up is needed for text-only books.

As your book takes shape, the publisher will send you e-drafts of the cover and the internals for your review and approval. Later they will send you a (sample) hard copy proof (a real book with covers) for your "final" review and approval.

While these steps usually cycle many times, they finally deliver to you a wonderful first volume that you will treasure as one more great first-time-happening in your life.

STEP 25
Agents - Publishers - POD

Once upon a time there were book publishers and suddenly agents appeared. Many books materialized. Some were great. Most were good. A few were not worth the read. Publishers and agents were happy and so were many good authors. So in big mansions - with two main doors - they threw huge parties.

New authors are never invited to these festivities but some show up anyway,. At one door they are stopped by the publisher's butler, "Do you have an agent? No? Sorry."

At the other door, they are stopped by the agent's butler. "Have you been published? No? Sorry."

Between these two doors there is a mail slot and some new authors drop their un-solicited manuscript into it. Alas, inside there is a conveyor belt that rolls from the mail slot to a slush pile out back.

The pile is scooped up by the trash crew every month.

Once in awhile, a new author has a friend of a friend who knows an agent or publisher and his or her manuscript gets "looked at" out of politeness or social obligation. A best-selling author may ask her agent to take a look at her boyfriend's story.

Question: What percentage of these favors result in a published book? Answer: Zip!

But wait, our challenge is bigger. When almanacs, newspapers and books first got introduced in 1875, they were widely read because what else was there to read…or do.

But today, we have newspapers, TV, video games, cell phones, epic films (in 3D), the internet, email, iPods, social networks, free blogs, You Tube, TED and thousands of other "pastimes" that compete for our eyes, our ears and our time.

Poof go the newspapers. Poof go big book advances. Poof go the music recording monopolies. Poof go the demand for books. Well, maybe half a poof. So any chance of getting into one of those big parties is close to…poof.

Newspapers, music, videos, movies, TV and even social conversation are migrating to e-distribution.

And so are books.

And that's good news for new authors because the electronic media has eased our access to book readers at a cost that is reasonable.

New authors have choices. They can look for an agent or look for a publisher or pay a printer to print and bind their book but the least expensive, most convenient way to launch a first book is through an e-Publisher that turns your manuscript (and illustrations) into a professionally finished book.

Your best bet is to use a Print-On-Demand (POD) publisher because they print only enough books to meet near term projected sales.

The expense for this launch is low compared to any other way.

For *The Sky Tree*, I used the POD publisher, Createspace, and I recommend you explore their services. They will supply you with a cost estimate for your book once its contents and size have been determined. They also can promote it, distribute it, ship it and administer the royalties.

Createspace is owned by Amazon so their offering can include listing your book on Amazon and Kindle or maybe later Apple's iPad.

STEP 26
Reference Books

As mentioned earlier, there are many excellent books on writing Romance, Mysteries, Thrillers, Sci-Fi, Adventure, Spy Novels, and Children's Stories. There are also books for illustrators, plotting, characters, grammar, punctuation, dialogue, style, voice and on and on.

But before you start reading, reading, reading, know this: the best way to absorb help from a skating instructor is to be skating. That's when learning really sinks in.

1W2W is effective because you learn *while* writing. After your first book is done, these other fine references will be much more meaningful to you. As I wrote *The Sky Tree*, I found the following three books most helpful:

> The Step-By-Step Guide to Self-Publishing for Profit – by C. Pinero and Nick Russell

Writing Children's Books for Dummies – by Lisa Romany Buccieri and Peter Economy

Perfect Pages - by Aaron Shepard

STEP 27
Our Legacies

The mission of *One Way To Write* is to inspire you to write a first book by simplifying the basic skills needed.

Simplifying any complex process requires highlighting the *important* techniques not *all* of the techniques and asking you to choose what to use. To me, books that cover all the techniques seem heavy on wisdom and light on inspiration.

I dodge any need to apologize for my short cut advice in this book because this is only *One Way To Write*.

My legacy is complete if I get one person to become a first time published author. Anything more than that…is gravy.

For all of us, first times are special and worth a try. Your Way To Write could be your legacy.

I'm sure you remember the day you learned how to swim, to skate and to drive. Those moments are still precious to you but not to many others.

Your first book is different because it's not only precious to you, your family and your friends but also to your readers for a long time.

That's your legacy and anything more than your first book…is gravy.

APPENDIX

Headlines for *The Sky Tree*

(Note that some names and events were changed for the book version)

*** 1 True Bees
Diza and Kiaz watch for birth of squirrel
Chakra falls from nest

*** 2 Minty
Kiaz announces Minty birth to forest
Minty spots crow nest
Diza warns Jewel about Kevin
Jewel tricks the bear

*** 3 Sky Tree
Minty sees the Sky Tree
Sky Tree becomes her dream

*** 4 Wrinkly
Kiaz sees Mika protect Minty
Mika learns to sneak-climb
Minty tells Mika about her dream
Minty shows Mika Sky Tree
Wrinkly encourages dream trip
Minty tells her mom and dad of trip

*** 5 Beaver Pond
They start on Sky Tree trip
They hear beaver chomping
They visit Penley and Glenda
Beavers have a water problem
Beavers warn trip is dangerous
    Purple ants
    Rage River
Beavers argue

*** 6 Sneak Climb
Sleep in Wrinkly after tickling it
Woodpecker wakens them
Play tag for a while.
Mika sneak-climbs and tags her
They resume trip and hear crow warning
Rabbit Nadia warns them of hawks
Nadia misses family and needs to
    plant thorny bushes so family will come back
Nadia tells of spider-web subway
She uses Blinky to lead them through tunnels

*** 7
They tree hop and climb Wrinkly
They get latest news from True bees
    about Jewel, Chakra, Nadia, hawks,
    but not Blinky
They sleep in cave that has mint leaves

*** 8 Purple Ants
Ricky woodpecker wakes them
Wrinkly warns them of river and ant party
Minty re-affirms dream trip
Wrinkly tells of rotten log "bridge."

*** 9 Sneak Swim
They creep close to river and encounter ant
Ant touches hiding Mika
They see ants guarding the rotten log
Minty has plan to sneak-climb to Grampa Wrinkly

*** 10 Drop Branch
They see and parade carring food
They slip into the river and sneak-swim
To Granpa Wrinkly

*** 11 Offering
They climb out on the "drop" branch
The wind and moon help them
Can't reach log, must decide go-no-go
They fall onto log
The ants hear them jump, look for them
Ants go to far side
The Sky Tree watches them, sends strong wind
They reach the island as log breaks and floats away

*** 12 Smoke Rings
They clean up to meet Sky Tree
Sky welcomes them and invites
    them up to wish branch

Minty squeezes water from Mika's tail as offering
They tell of their trip
Sky Tree asks what is their wish
Minty trades her cloud dream for helping
    her friends with a "sneak-wish"
The wind, clouds and lightning deliver her wish
The Sky Tree has a surprise for them
Sky Tree brings the clouds down to the
    wish branch so they can be in the clouds.
The True bees flap their wings –
    corkscrews in the mist
Minty closes her eyes and breathes in the clouds
Mika toys with blowing smoke rings

*** 13 Epilogue
Minty and Mika go home
The True Bees
Nadia
Beavers
Chakra
Kevin

Inside back cover
    Blank

Outside back cover
    Blurb
    Author Bio and Pic

www.ingramcontent.com/pod-product-compliance
Lightning Source LLC
Chambersburg PA
CBHW071508040426
42444CB00008B/1552